Contents

Summary of issues

Q.1.   Does the Human Rights Act 1998 provide a sufficient legislative framework for tackling religious discrimination?

Q.2.   Should there be a non-statutory voluntary code of practice on religious discrimination?

Q.3.   If new legislation is required, should this be by way of amendment to the Race Relations Act, or by a separate Religious Discrimination Act, or as part of a single Equality Act covering all grounds of unlawful discrimination?

Q.4.   On what grounds should the legislation prohibit discrimination?
   • Religion
   • Religious Belief
   • Religion or Belief

Q.5.   Should the legislation cover the lack of all or any religious belief? If so, should this be clearly stated in the legislation?

Q.6.   What should be included as essential elements in any definition of religion?

Q.7.   Should there be a list of officially recognised religions? What would be the criteria and the process by which religions gained official recognition?

Q.8.   Is a definition of religion a necessary pre-requisite for legislation to tackle religious discrimination or should this be left for the courts to develop?

Q.9.   What should be included as essential elements to any definition of belief?

Q.10.   Is a definition of belief a necessary pre-requisite to tackle discrimination on the grounds of religion or belief or should this be left for the courts to develop?

Q.11.   Should the legislation prohibit (a) direct discrimination, (b) indirect discrimination, and (c) harassment?

Q.12.   What should be the definition of indirect discrimination?

Q.13.   Should indirect discrimination be combined with a duty to make reasonable adjustments?

Q.14.   What areas of activity should be covered by legislation on religious discrimination?

Q.15.   Should legislation prohibiting religious discrimination cover all public authorities, including schools and education authorities?

Q.16.   Should there be a general defence of justification for direct discrimination or should there be only specific exemptions?

Q.17.   If there are to be specific exemptions should they be worded in broad terms, and if so what should the formulation be? For example, should there be an exemption where belonging to a particular faith is a genuine occupational qualification or requirement?

Q.18.   Alternatively, should there be a list of specific posts that are exempt from legislation prohibiting religious discrimination? If so, what posts should be included in that list?

Q.19.   Should there be a general exemption that allows particular persons or bodies to discriminate in employment where it is necessary to do so in order to comply with the organisation's religious ethos?

Q.20.   To whom should this exemption apply?

Q.21.   Should there be an exemption allowing discrimination by religious bodies in the provision of goods, services, facilities and education?

Q.22.   Should there be an exemption allowing religious bodies to discriminate on other grounds, such as sex or sexual orientation, where this is appropriate and necessary to comply with the doctrines of the religion or to avoid offending the religious susceptibilities of a significant number of its followers?

Q.23.   Are there any grounds on which such bodies should not be allowed to discriminate irrespective of the doctrines of their religion, such as race?

Q.24.   What approach should be taken in deciding:
- If an employee's practice is a manifestation of a religion or belief?
- If an employer's practice or policy conflicts with the employee's religious practice

Q.25.   What factors should be taken into account in determining if the duty to accommodate has been complied with?

Q.26.   On whom should the duty to accommodate fall?

Q.27.   How should employers accommodate religious observance?

Q.28.   In relation to which religious practices or observances are questions of reasonable accommodation likely to arise and how should such practices and observances be accommodated?

Q.29.   Should there be a duty on public authorities to promote religious equality?

Q.30.   Should there be a duty on private sector employers to promote religious equality?

Q.31.   Should the legislation allow positive action to ensure equal treatment for religious groups?

Q.32.   Should there be an organisation with responsibility for enforcement of religious discrimination legislation, and if so who should have this responsibility –
- The Commission for Racial Equality
- A new Commission for Religious Relations
- A single Equality Commission dealing with all grounds of discrimination
- A Human Rights Commission?

Q.33.   What other enforcement measures are required?

Abbreviations

CRE	Commission for Racial Equality
DDA	Disability Discrimination Act
DfEE	Department for Education and Employment
DRC	Disability Rights Commission
EAT	Employment Appeals Tribunal
ECHR	European Convention for the Protection of Human Rights and Fundamental Freedoms
ECJ	European Court of Justice
ECNI	Equality Commission for Northern Ireland
EEOC	Equal Employment Opportunity Commission
EOC	Equal Opportunities Commission
FEA	Fair Employment Act 1989
FEC	Fair Employment Commission
FETO	Fair Employment and Treatment (Northern Ireland) Order 1998
GOQ	Genuine Occupational Qualification
HREOC	Human Rights and Equal Opportunities Commission
HRA	Human Rights Act
ICCPR	International Covenant on Civil and Political Rights 1966
ICESCR	International Covenant on Economic, Social and Cultural Rights 1966
IPPR	Institute of Public Policy Research
NIA	Northern Ireland Act 1998
RRA	Race Relations Act 1976
SDA	Sex Discrimination Act 1975

Introduction

This paper was commissioned by the Home Office from the Cambridge Centre for Public Law. Its purpose is to identify and examine the main options available to policy makers and legislators for tackling religious discrimination in Great Britain. It takes into consideration the implications of the recent anti-discrimination directives under Article 13 of the EC Treaty; the Human Rights Act 1998 (HRA) and the European Convention for the Protection of Human Rights and Fundamental Freedoms (ECHR); the current race relations regime, including the Race Relations (Amendment) Act 2000; as well as other relevant UK legislation and practice. Where appropriate reference is made to provisions in other EU Member States, the USA and Commonwealth countries.

The focus is on employment and the provision of goods, facilities and services, including education. Although issues of crime, public order and constitutional matters are highly significant, these were specifically excluded from our remit and are not discussed in this paper. Nor does the paper enter the debate on whether there is a need for legislation or other policies to tackle religious discrimination. These latter issues are considered in other research commissioned by the Home Office.

The present paper draws on the Report of the Independent Review of the Enforcement of UK Anti-Discrimination Legislation.[1] That review made fifty-three detailed recommendations for reform of discrimination law and policy as a whole. This paper aims to inform the debate on religious discrimination by reviewing the main options, but does not make any specific recommendations.

Cambridge
12 January 2001

---

1   B. Hepple, M. Coussey, T. Choudhury, *Equality: A New Framework – The Report of the Independent Review of the Enforcement of UK Anti-Discrimination Legislation,* (Oxford, Hart Publishing, 2000).

1.1 The policy options for tackling religious discrimination need to be placed within the wider context of existing measures at national and European level.

(A) Protection from religious discrimination under the current law in the UK

(i) Northern Ireland

1.2 At present there is explicit protection from religious discrimination only in Northern Ireland, where the legislation, reflecting the particular sectarian issues in that jurisdiction, is directed primarily at relations between the established Protestant and Roman Catholic communities. *The Northern Ireland Act 1998* prohibits discrimination by the government and public bodies on the grounds of religious belief or political opinion. Discrimination on these grounds in employment is prohibited by the *Fair Employment and Treatment (Northern Ireland) Order 1998 (FETO)*[2] which replaces the *Fair Employment (Northern Ireland) Acts 1976 and 1989* and extends the protection to cover the provision of goods, services and facilities.

1.3 The legislation takes a proactive approach to tackling religious discrimination. Under the *Northern Ireland Act* it is unlawful for a public authority to "discriminate, or to aid or incite another person to discriminate, against a person or class of persons on the grounds of religious belief or political opinion"[3] Furthermore there is a duty on public authorities to promote equality of opportunity:[4]

(1) A public authority shall in carrying out its functions relating to Northern Ireland have due regard to the need to promote equality of opportunity –

    (a) between persons of different religious belief, political opinion, racial group, age, marital status or sexual orientation;

(2) Without prejudice to its obligations under subsection (1), a public authority shall in carrying out its functions relating to Northern Ireland have regard to the desirability of promoting good relations between persons of different religious belief, political opinion or racial group.

---

2 No. 3162 (N.I. 21) (hereafter FETO).
3 Northern Ireland Act 1998, s.76 (hereafter NIA).
4 NIA, s.75.

1.4   The weight of the obligation to have "due regard" to the need to promote equality of opportunity remains uncertain. Professor Christopher McCrudden argues that this is not just a statutory duty but a "constitutional duty and should therefore be accorded considerable weight".[5] The duty goes beyond avoiding discrimination. Public bodies are required actively to seek ways to encourage greater equality of opportunity through their policy development.[6]

1.5   The FETO requires private sector employers with more than 10 full time employees in Northern Ireland to register with the Equality Commission (ECNI).[7] Registered employers and public authorities are required to prepare and serve each year on the Commission a monitoring return to enable the composition of the work force, including part-time employees, in terms of membership of the Catholic and Protestant communities to be ascertained. These employers are also required to serve a monitoring return to enable the composition of applicants for employment to be ascertained. The legislation allows affirmative action policies to be followed in relation to access to training,[8] in the practice relating to the selection of workers for redundancy,[9] and in measures taken to encourage applications from under-represented communities.[10] "Affirmative action" is defined in section 4 as:

(1)   action designed to secure fair participation in employment by members of the Protestant, or members of the Roman Catholic community, in Northern Ireland by means including-

(a)   the adoption of practices encouraging such participation; and

(b)   the modification of practices that have or may have the effect of restricting or discouraging such participation.

It is further provided that:

5(5)   Any reference to the promotion of equality of opportunity includes a reference to affirmative actions and, accordingly, any reference to action for promoting equality of opportunity includes a reference to affirmative action.

---

5   C. McCrudden, "The Equality of Opportunity Duty in the Northern Ireland Act 1998: An Analysis", in *The Equality Provision of the Good Friday Agreement and the NI Act*, (Committee for the Administration of Justice, 1999), at p.14.
6   Ibid.
7   FETO, art. 48.
8   FETO, art. 72.
9   FETO, art. 73.
10   FETO, art. 77.

Section 7 of FETO places a duty on the Equality Commission to promote affirmative action.

1.6   The House of Commons Northern Ireland Affairs Committee reported in 1999 that:

> The extent to which employers have complied with the regulatory requirements of the legislation appears to be impressive...The [Fair Employment Commission (predecessor to the Equality Commission)] reported a high level of compliance by employers with their statutory duties of monitoring, submitting monitoring returns, and periodically reviewing their employment practices. It also reported that there have been considerable improvements in equality-based employment practices in recent years.[11]

> The Committee also reported that there had been reductions in employment segregation, in the under representation of the Catholic community overall and of Protestant and Roman Catholic communities in specific areas, and in the unemployment differentials between the communities.[12]

(ii) The Race Relations Act

1.7   In Great Britain the Race Relations Act 1976 (RRA),[13] which prohibits discrimination on "racial grounds", defined as "colour, race, nationality, or ethnic or national origins", makes no express reference to religious discrimination.[14] However, ways have been found to provide limited protection under the Act to some religious groups which have the characteristics of an ethnic group. In this way protection has been offered to Sikhs[15] and Jewish people.[16] The recognition of a religious community as an ethnic group provides them with protection from both direct and indirect discrimination. In the case of Mandla v Dowell Lee the House of Lords accepted that ethnic origin is a wider concept than race and identified several characteristics relevant to identifying an ethnic group.[17] The two essential characteristics are:

---

11   House of Commons Northern Ireland Affairs Committee Fourth Report (1999), *The Operation of the Fair Employment (Northern Ireland) Act 1989: Ten Years On,* Session 1998-99 HC 98, at para 48.
12   Ibid. at para 37.
13   Legislation prohibiting racial discrimination was introduced into Northern Ireland in 1997 by the Race Relations (Northern Ireland) Order 1997, (SI 869 (NI 6)).
14   An attempt to include religious discrimination in the 1976 Act failed: HC Standing Committee A, 29 April 1976 and 4 May 1976, cols. 84-118.
15   *Mandla v Dowell Lee* [1983] 2 AC 548.
16   *Seide v Gillette Industries Ltd* [1980] IRLR 427.
17   See n.15.

- A long shared history, which the group is conscious of as distinguishing it from other groups; and
- A cultural tradition of its own, including family and social customs and manners, often but not necessarily associated with religious observance.

Five other characteristics were identified as relevant but not essential:

- Either a common geographical origin, or descent from small number of common ancestors;
- A common language, not necessarily peculiar to the group;
- A common religion different from that of neighbouring groups or from the general community around it;
- Being a minority or being an oppressed or a dominant group within a larger community.

Under these criteria Gypsies have been found to constitute a racial group by virtue of their shared history, geographical origins, distinct customs, language derived from Romany and a common culture.[18] On the other hand Muslims,[19] Rastafarians[20] and Jehovah's Witnesses[21] have been held not to constitute racial or ethnic groups.

1.8   A second way of bringing religious groups within the ambit of the RRA has been through the concept of indirect discrimination. Actions taken by an employer causing detriment to Muslims as a class, such as refusal to allow time off work for religious holidays, might be held to constitute indirect racial discrimination against those from an ethnic or national origin that is predominantly Muslim.[22] This does not help Muslims who come from a country where Muslims are in a minority. The limitation of using indirect race discrimination to tackle religious discrimination is highlighted in the decision of the tribunal in *Safouane &*

---

18   *Commission for Racial Equality v Dutton* [1989] IRLR 8.
19   Tariq v Young Case 247738/88, EOR Discrimination Case Law Digest No. 2; cf K.S.Dobe and S.S.Chhokar (2000) 4 Int.*Journal of Discrimination and the Law* pp.369-86 who argue that the criteria in Mandla v Lee are sufficiently broad to recognise British Muslims as an "ethnic group".
20   *Crown Suppliers (Property Services Agency) v Dawkins* [1993] ICR 517.
21   *Lovell-Badge v Norwich City College of Further and Higher Education*, Case no: 1502237/97, (Spring 1999) 39 EOR Discrimination Case Law Digest, 4.
22   *J H Walker Ltd v Hussain* [1996] IRLR 11 EAT. Other cases where the indirect discrimination provisions have been used include: *CRE v. Precision Manufacturing Services Ltd.*,10 October 1991, Case No 4106/91, (Summer 1992) 12 EOR Case Law Digest, 8; *Yassin v. Northwest Homecare* (Spring 1994) 19 EOR Case Law Digest 2.

Bouterfas (1996).[23] In that case two Muslim complainants were dismissed for doing prayers during their breaks. The tribunal held that the acts did not constitute indirect racial discrimination because the applicants belonged to the same North African ethnic Arab minority as the respondents and that they had a good record of employing staff from a diversity of backgrounds. Even if a finding of indirect race discrimination is made, the legislation does not at present allow for an award of compensation to be made in cases of indirect race discrimination where there is no intention to discriminate.[24]

1.9   Attempts have also been made to use the *Sex Discrimination Act* 1975(SDA) to provide protection against some aspects of religious discrimination. In the case of *Sardar v McDonalds* (1998) a Muslim female complainant was successful in a claim of indirect sex discrimination after she was dismissed for wearing a scarf to cover her hair.[25]

1.10   Attempts have been made to introduce religious discrimination legislation. In 1998 John Austin MP introduced a Private Member's Bill in the House of Commons to prohibit religious discrimination in employment and in the provision of goods, services and facilities.[26] The Bill made no progress due to lack of time. The House of Lord also discussed the issue of religious discrimination in 1999 in a debate initiated by Lord Ahmed.[27] A Race Relations (Religious Discrimination) Bill was introduced by Lord Ahmed and given a second reading in the House of Lords in June 2000.[28]

(iii) The Human Rights Act

1.11   The "bringing home" of rights under the *European Convention for the Protection of Human Rights and Fundamental Freedoms (ECHR)* by the *Human Rights Act 1998 (HRA)* provides the first express protection from religious discrimination in the UK outside Northern Ireland. The Act provides for the enforcement in UK courts and tribunals of rights secured by the ECHR (so-called "convention rights").

---

23   *Safouane & Bouterfas v. Joseph Ltd and Hannah* [1996] Case No. 12506/95/LS & 12569/95, cited in The Association of Muslim Lawyers, *Paper for the Commission on British Muslims – Seminar on Religious Discrimination*, (December 1999), p. 2.

24   RRA, s.57(3).

25   Cited in The Association of Muslim Lawyers, (1999), see n. 22 at p. 2. *See also Khanum v. IBC Vehicles Ltd.*, Case No. 1200058/97, (Autumn 1998) 37 EOR Case Law Digest 3.

26   HC Deb, 3 March 1998, col. 859.

27   HL Deb, 28 October 1999, c. 454-478.

28   HL Deb, 7 June 2000, col. 1189-1209.

The Act makes it unlawful for public authorities to act in a way which is incompatible with convention rights, although such an act is not unlawful if it is the effect of primary legislation. Individuals and organisations which have been directly affected will be able to challenge the act or omission in the courts. They may do so in legal actions which the authority takes against them (e.g. criminal prosecutions) or by way of judicial review of executive decisions. Damages or other appropriate relief may be awarded against a public authority which is found to have acted contrary to a convention right. So far as it is possible to do so, primary legislation and subordinate legislation must be read and given effect to in a way which is compatible with convention rights. If a court determines that it is impossible to interpret an Act of Parliament in a way which is compatible with convention rights, a formal declaration of incompatibility may be made, and it is then for the Government and Parliament to decide whether or not to amend it. The courts are, however, entitled to strike down or set aside secondary legislation which is incompatible with convention rights. Apart from the HRA, the devolution legislation requires the devolved administrations and institutions in Scotland, Northern Ireland, and Wales to act in a way that is compatible with convention rights.[29]

1.12 Articles 9 and 14 of the Convention and Article 2 of Protocol 1 are the most relevant in relation to religious discrimination. Article 9 contains two elements. The first is a right to freedom of thought, conscience and religion. This includes freedom to change one's religion or belief. This is guaranteed by the convention without qualification. The second element is the freedom, either alone or in community with others and in public or in private, to manifest one's religion or belief. This is limited to acts of worship, teaching, practice and observance. It is also subject to limitation in accordance with Article 9(2). A limitation must be "prescribed by law" and "necessary in a democratic society, in the interests of public safety, for the protection of public order, health and morals, or for the protection of the rights and freedoms of others".

1.13 Article 9 requires, firstly, negative protection from interference by the state unless the interference falls within Article 9(2). Secondly, there is a positive obligation on the state to ensure the peaceful enjoyment of the rights under Article 9. The European Court of Human Rights has said that there is no obligation on the state to protect citizens from offence to their beliefs caused by other private individuals. However, the Court has recognised that "in extreme cases the effect of particular

---

29   There are, however, significant differences of detail in this regard between the provisions of the Scotland Act 1998, the Northern Ireland Act 1998, and the Government of Wales Act 1998: see generally, Lord Hope of Craighead, "Devolution and Human Rights" [1998] *European Human Rights Law Review 367.*

methods of opposing or denying religious beliefs can be such as to inhibit those who hold such beliefs from exercising their freedom to hold and express them."[30]

1.14   Section 13 of the HRA makes special provision for freedom of religion. It requires that any court or tribunal determining any question arising under the HRA which might affect the exercise by a religious organisation (itself or its members collectively) of the convention right to freedom of thought, conscience and religion must have "particular regard to the importance of that right". The Home Secretary explained, at the Committee stage of the Bill,[31] that the purpose of this clause was to reassure religious organisations "against the Bill being used to intrude upon genuinely religious beliefs or practices based on their beliefs." In particular, the clause was designed "to bring out the point that Article 9 rights attach not only to individuals, but to Churches." There is Convention jurisprudence to this effect, and section 13 emphasises this to the courts. According to the Home Secretary, "the intention is to focus the courts' attention in any proceedings on the view generally held by the Church in question, and on its interest in protecting the integrity of the common faith of its members against attack, whether by outsiders or by individual dissidents. That is a significant protection." The term "religious organisation" is not defined in either the HRA or in the jurisprudence of the European Court of Human Rights. The Home Secretary was confident, on the advice of parliamentary counsel, that the term is flexible enough to cover cases involving religious charities where Church issues form a backdrop of the case, and is not tied to circumstances in which a religious organisation is directly involved, as a body, in the court proceedings. "If a case is brought against a charity, and a charity can show that what it is doing is to maintain and practise the religious beliefs which it shares with its parent Church, we consider that the new clause 9 [now section 13] would come into play so as to ensure that due consideration is given to those beliefs."[32]

1.15   Article 9 does not provide for equal treatment. The principle of non-discrimination is dealt with only in Article 14 of the ECHR. This provides that the exercise of the rights and freedoms set forth in the convention must be secured without discrimination on any ground including religion, political or other opinion.[33] This is not a free-standing right against discrimination on grounds of religion or opinion. It is ancillary to other convention rights. No claim of religious discrimination can

---

30   *Otto-Preminger Institute v Austria* (1994) 19 *European Human Rights Reports* 34 at para.47; cf. *Choudhury v United Kingdom* (1991) 12 *Human Rights Law Journal* 172.

31   HC Debates, 20 May 1998,cols. 1023-24.

32   Ibid.,col.1024.

33   'The enjoyment of the rights and freedoms set forth in this Convention shall be secured without discrimination on any ground such as sex, race, colour, language, religion, political or other opinion, national or social origin, association with a national minority, property, birth or other status.'

be made except in conjunction with one of the specified convention rights. The European Court of Human Rights has held that there may be a violation of Article 14 in conjunction with another convention right even if there is no violation of that other Article taken alone.[34] Nevertheless, in the absence of a convention right, there can be no recourse to Article 14. In order to remedy this, the Council of Europe has recently adopted Protocol No. 12 to the Convention. Article 1 of this Protocol provides for a general prohibition on discrimination:

(1)   The enjoyment of any right set forth by law shall be secured without discrimination in any ground such as sex, race, colour, language, *religion, political or other opinion*, national or social origin, association with a national minority, property, birth or other status.[emphasis added].

(2)   No one shall be discriminated against by any public authority on any ground such as those mentioned in paragraph 1.

1.16   According to the Explanatory Memorandum prepared by the Council of Europe, the expression "any right set forth by law", is meant to cover (i) the enjoyment of any right specifically granted to an individual by national law; (ii) the enjoyment of a right which may be inferred from a clear obligation of a public authority under national law, i.e. where a public authority is obliged under national law to behave in a particular manner; (iii) the exercise of a discretionary power by a public authority (e.g. in granting certain subsidies); and (iv) any other act or omission by a public authority (e.g. behaviour of law enforcement officers). The prime objective of Article 1 is to embody a negative obligation on public authorities not to discriminate; it does not impose a general positive obligation to take measures to prevent or prohibit all instances of discrimination between private persons. On the other hand, the duty to "secure", under the first paragraph of Article 1, might entail a positive obligation where there is a clear gap in protection from discrimination under domestic law. In other words, it would oblige a ratifying state to secure protection against discrimination on all the proscribed grounds, including religion.

1.17   Protocol No.12 was signed by 25 of the Council's member states at the Rome Conference on 4 November 2000, and will come into force when 10 members have ratified it.[35] The UK has not signed the protocol. In reply to a parliamentary question, Lord Bassam of Brighton stated:

---

34   *Belgian Linguistics Case* (No.2) (1968) 1 EHRR 252.

35   The following states have so far signed Protocol No. 12: Austria, Belgium, Cyprus, Czech Republic, Estonia, Finland, Georgia, Germany, Greece, Hungary, Iceland, Ireland, Italy, Latvia, Liechtenstein, Luxembourg, Moldova, the Netherlands, Portugal, Romania, Russia, San Marino, Slovakia, "the former Yugoslav Republic of Macedonia" and Ukraine.

"The Government did not sign Protocol 12 when it was opened for signature in Rome on 4 November and have no present plans to do so, but they have not indefinitely ruled out signature and ratification. They will keep their position under consideration in the light of the interpretation of the protocol BY the European Court of Human Rights."[36]

The Government has stated that the protocol is "too general and open-ended" and that "it does not make clear whether 'rights set forth by law' include international as well as national law".[37] They are concerned that "the European Court of Human Rights might hold that a right set out in an international agreement, but not incorporated into United Kingdom law is covered by Protocol 12".[38] Furthermore they argue that it "does not make provision for positive measures; and it does not follow the case law of the European Court of Human Rights in allowing objective and reasonably justified distinctions."[39] They believe that the preamble, which provides that states can take measures to promote full and effective equality provided that there is an objective and reasonable justification for those measures, "does not have the same force as the substantive provision in the protocol itself…[which] does not provide any exception".[40] They also note that "new rights are not necessarily cost free (especially when they are economic, social and cultural rights) and may affect the rights of others, as many rights have to be balanced against each other."[41] The heads of the CRE, EOC and DRC, among others, believe that these arguments are misconceived and have urged the Government to sign and ratify Protocol No.12.[42] If the Protocol is signed and ratified by the UK, the Secretary of State could amend the HRA 1998 to as to reflect its effect, subject to approval by Parliament. This would give rise to remedies in UK courts and tribunals against public authorities in respect of religious discrimination in respect of all legal rights and not only those rights which are guaranteed by the Convention. For example, access to employment in the civil service is not a convention right and so it appears that religious discrimination against applicants would not at present be protected. Protocol No.12 would provide a remedy in such circumstances. However, the new Protocol does not apply to the acts of private bodies.

---

36   HL , 9 November 2000, WA 174 .
37   HL, 11 October 2000, WA 37.
38   HL, 23 October 2000, WA 14.
39   HL, 11 October 2000, WA 37.
40   HL, 23 October 2000, WA 14.
41   HL, 25 October 2000, WA 45.
42   The Times, 3 November 2000.

1.18   Article 2 of Protocol No.1 to the ECHR touches on the issue of religion and education. It states that:

No person shall be denied the right to education. In exercise of any functions which it assumes in relation to education and to teaching, the State shall respect the right of parents to ensure such education and teaching in conformity with their own religious and philosophical convictions.

The UK has entered the following reservation in relation to this article:

… in view of certain provisions of the Education Acts in the United Kingdom, the principle affirmed in the second sentence of Article 2 is accepted by the United Kingdom only in so far as it is compatible with the provision of efficient instruction and training, and the avoidance of unreasonable public expenditure.

The implications of the HRA will be discussed in more detail below in considering the different legislative and policy options for tackling religious discrimination.

(B) The European Union

1.19   The most immediate pressure for legislation and policies for tackling religious discrimination comes from the European Union. Traditionally, the law of the European Community (EC) has provided protection only against discrimination on the basis of sex[43] and (for EU citizens) nationality[44]. The European Court of Justice has stated (in staff cases) that the right to non-discrimination on religious grounds is a fundamental right to be protected by Community law,[45] but prior to the Treaty of Amsterdam there was no express power for the Community to deal with racial or religious discrimination. Article 13 of the EC Treaty, as introduced by the Treaty of Amsterdam, puts an end to the long debate about Community competence on anti-discrimination matters. It provides a legal basis for the Council, acting unanimously, on a proposal from the Commission and after consultation with the European Parliament, to take "appropriate action" to combat discrimination based on "sex, racial or ethnic origin, *religion or belief*, disability, age or sexual orientation".

---

43   Art. 141 EC (Ex. Art. 119 EEC). See also Equal Pay Directive Dir. 75/117 EEC; Equal Treatment Directive 1976 Dir. 76/207 EEC; and Equal Treatment in Social Security Directive 79/7 EEC; Burden of Proof Directive 1997 Dir. 97/80/EC.
44   Art. 12 EC (Ex Art. 6 EC).
45   Prais v. EC Council, case 130/75 (1976) ECR 1589.

1.20   On 29 June 2000 the Council adopted Directive 2000/43/EC[46] implementing the principle of equal treatment between persons irrespective of race or ethnic origin ("the race directive"). On 27 November 2000 Directive 2000/78/EC[47] was adopted establishing a general framework for equal treatment in employment and occupation without discrimination "on grounds of *religion or belief*, disability, age or sexual orientation" ("the employment directive"). The race directive is wider in scope than the employment directive because, in addition to employment, it covers social protection, social advantages, goods and services. The race directive must be implemented by the UK by 19 July 2003, and the employment directive by 2 December 2003 in respect of religion or belief. The Council has also adopted a Community action programme to combat discrimination in the period 2001 to 2006.[48]

1.21   The final versions of the race and employment directives differ in significant respects from the drafts which were examined by the House of Lords Select Committee on the European Union in May 2000.[49] In a further Report, after the adoption of the directives, the Select Committee renewed their criticisms of the structure and some other aspects of the employment directive.[50] The issues arising from the employment directive are among the subjects of this paper. The directive lays down only "minimum requirements". The UK is free to introduce or maintain provisions which are more favourable to equal treatment than those in the directive.[51]

1.22   The interaction between the Article 13 employment directive, the ECHR and the HRA is complex. Article 6(1) of the Treaty of European Union (TEU) provides that the "Union is founded on the principles of liberty, democracy, respect for human rights and fundamental freedoms, and the rule of law, principles which are common to the Member States", and Article 6(2) states that "the Union shall respect fundamental rights, as guaranteed by the [ECHR] and as they result from the constitutional traditions common to the Member States, as general principles of Community law." This confirms the long-standing practice of the European Court of Justice in using the ECHR as an embodiment of the general principles

46   OJ L 180/22, 19.7.2000.
47   OJ L 303/16, 2.12.2000.
48   OJ L 303/23, 2.12.2000.
49   House of Lords, Select Committee on the European Union, Session 1999-2000, Ninth Report, EU Proposals to Combat Discrimination, HL 68. The report was debated in the House of Lords in June, see: HL Deb, 30 June 2000, cols. 1178-1235.
50   House of Lords, Select Committee on the European Union, Session 2000-01, Fourth Report, The EU Framework Directive on Discrimination, HL 13.
51   Art.8(1). Under no circumstances may the protection already afforded by Member States in fields covered by the directive be reduced: Art.8(2).

common to the Member States. The recent EU Charter of Fundamental Rights, proclaimed at the Nice European Council on 7 December 2000, while not directly legally binding, may also be seen by the European Court of Justice as a source of inspiration which the Community institutions and the Member States when implementing Community obligations must respect.[52] Article 10 of the EU Charter follows Article 9 of the ECHR on freedom of thought, conscience and religion, and Article 13 has a free-standing provision, along the lines of Protocol No.12 to the ECHR, which prohibits discrimination on grounds, among others, of "religion or belief". The overall effect of the TEU, the EU Charter, and the HRA will be to require the EC employment directive to be implemented so as to be compatible with the rights set out in the ECHR.

(C) Legislation in other EU States

1.23   There are constitutional provisions relating to religious equality in all other Member States (see Appendix 1), but (according to information provided by the European Commission) there appears to be specific anti-discrimination legislation in only two countries, the Republic of Ireland and the Netherlands.

(i) Republic of Ireland

1.24   The *Employment Equality Act* 1998 prohibits discrimination on the grounds, *inter alia*, of religious belief. The Act covers discrimination by employers, with regard to access to employment, conditions of employment, training and promotion.[53] It also covers discrimination by employment agencies,[54] as well as discrimination in vocational training,[55] in collective agreements[56] and by professional bodies and trade unions.[57] Sections 36 and 37 set out the general exemptions including an exemption allowing discrimination by religious, educational and medical institutions run by religious bodies, or by bodies whose objectives include the provision of services in an environment which promotes certain religious values, where it gives more favourable treatment on grounds of religion in order to maintain the religious ethos of the institution or it takes action to prevent an employee or prospective employee from undermining the religious ethos of the institution.

---

52   This is the view of the European Commission COM (2000) 644, 11 October 2000, but the UK Government has emphasised that "it should have no legal status, and we do not intend it to": HC Deb.,11 December 2000, col.354 (Prime Minister).

53   Employment Equality Act 1998 (hereafter EEA), s. 8.

54   EEA, s. 11.

55   EEA, s. 12.

56   EEA, s. 9.

57   EEA, s. 13.

1.25   Discrimination on the grounds of religious belief in the provision of goods, services and facilities is covered by the *Equal Status Act 2000*. There is an exemption allowing discrimination on the grounds of religion in relation to goods and services provided for a religious purpose.[58] There are also exemptions from the prohibition of discrimination in the disposal of premises and the provision of accommodation where "any premises or accommodation are reserved for the use of persons in a particular category of persons for a religious purpose"[59] Discrimination is permitted in the membership of clubs where the principal purpose of the club is to meet the needs of persons of a particular religious belief or persons who have no religious belief.[60] An educational establishment is held not to discriminate on grounds of religion if it is set up to provide training to ministers of religion and admits students of only one gender or religious belief. A school is held not to discriminate where its objective is to provide education in an environment that promotes certain religious values and it admits persons of a particular religious denomination.[61]

(ii) The Netherlands

1.26   The Dutch Constitution protects both freedom of religion and at article 1 a right to equality. The Equal Treatment Act 1984 prohibits the imposition of direct or indirect distinctions in employment on the grounds of religious or other belief.[62] The Act covers employment, the provision of goods, services and facilities, with particular reference to housing, education, health, welfare, sport and culture.

(D) Legislation in other common law countries

(i) United States of America

1.27   The first amendment of the US constitution provides that Congress may neither establish religion nor prohibit its free exercise. Title VII of the Civil Rights Act 1964 prohibits religious discrimination in employment and in public accommodation, facilities and education. It requires the employer to make reasonable attempts to accommodate the religious practices of employees.

---

58   *Equal Status Act 2000* (hereafter ESA), s. 5(2)(e).
59   ESA, s. 6(5).
60   ESA, s. 9(1)(a).
61   ESA, s. 7(3).
62   Equal Treatment Act 1984, s. 178 and 189 . The Dutch High Court has also given rulings on the scope of Art.9 ECHR: see B.C.Laubaschagne, "Religious Freedom and newly established Religions in Dutch law", (1997) 44 *Netherlands International Law Review* 168.

(ii) Australia

1.28   At the Commonwealth level the *Human Rights and Equal Opportunities Commission Act 1986* establishes the Commission and gives it responsibility for observing Australia's international human rights obligations under seven treaties including the Declaration on the Elimination of All Forms of Intolerance and of Discrimination Based on Religion or Belief. Several Australian states also have legislation prohibiting religious discrimination within their general equal opportunities or anti-discrimination legislation (see Appendix 1).

(iii) Canada

1.29   The Canadian *Charter of Rights and Freedoms* took effect in 1982 as an amendment to the constitution. Article 2(a) of the Canadian Charter of Rights protects the fundamental right to freedom of conscience and religion, while article 2(b) protect the fundamental freedoms of thought, belief, opinion and expression. Furthermore, article 15(1) provides that every individual has the right to equal protection and benefit of the law without discrimination based on religion. These freedoms and rights are 'subject only to such reasonable limits prescribed by law as can be demonstrably justified in a free and democratic society'.

1.30   At the federal level the *Canadian Human Rights Act* 1985 prohibits discrimination on the grounds of religion in all federal and federally regulated organisations. The provinces and territories have similar laws forbidding discrimination in their areas of jurisdiction. Complaints are handled by the Canadian Human Rights Commission and a number of provincial commissions, (see Appendix 1).

(iv) New Zealand

1.31   Section 13 of New Zealand's *Bill of Rights Act 1990* protects the freedom of thought, conscience, religion and belief. Section 15 protects the right to manifest that religion or belief in worship, observance, practice or teaching. Section 20 makes provision for the protection of minority religious rights.

1.32   The New Zealand *Human Rights Act 1993* prohibits discrimination on the grounds of religion or belief within the areas of employment, accommodation, education and goods and services.

(v) South Africa

1.33   The South African Constitution guarantees "freedom of religion, conscience and belief", and also prohibits discrimination on these grounds. This has been given effect by the *Promotion of Equality and Prevention of Unfair Discrimination Act, No.4 of 2000*, which prohibits unfair discrimination on a number of grounds including "religion, conscience, belief" and "culture". This covers goods, facilities and services, including education and employment. There appears to be some overlap with the earlier *Employment Equity Act No.55 of 1998*, which prohibits unfair discrimination in employment on the same grounds and also "political opinion". The *Employment Equity Act* also requires affirmative action measures to be taken by employers.

(E) International Human Rights Law

1.34   It is clear that international human rights law creates an obligation on the UK to provide protection against religious discrimination. The UK has ratified the International Covenant on Civil and Political Rights (the ICCPR) which contains two articles prohibiting religious discrimination: articles 2(1) and 26. Article 2(1) states that:

Each State Party...undertakes to respect and to ensure to all individuals within its territory and subject to its jurisdiction the rights recognised in the present Covenant, without distinction of any kind, such as race, colour, sex language, *religion*, political or other opinion, national or social origin, property birth or other status.

It requires State Parties "to take the necessary steps...to adopt such laws or other measures as may be necessary to give effect to the rights recognised" in the Covenant.[63] This includes measures necessary to ensure enjoyment of the rights under the Covenant without discrimination. A more comprehensive right of equality is contained in Article 26, which provides that:

All persons are equal before the law and are entitled without any discrimination to the equal protection of the law. In this respect, the law shall prohibit any discrimination and guarantee to all persons equal and effective protection against discrimination on any ground such as race, colour, sex, language, *religion*, political or other opinion, national or social origin, property, birth or other status.

1.35   As a counterpart to the civil and political rights in the ICCPR, the International Covenant on Economic, Social and Cultural Rights (ICESCR), also ratified by the UK, attempts to give effect to the economic, social and cultural rights mentioned in

---

63   ICCPR, art. 2(2)

the Universal Declaration. The non-discrimination and equality clauses of the Covenant are contained in Article 2(2). State Parties must guarantee the rights in the Covenant "without discrimination of any kind as to...religion".[64]

1.36   In 1999 the Government ratified the ILO Convention No.111 of 1958 concerning discrimination in respect of employment and occupation.[65] The Convention prohibits discrimination on the grounds of, *inter alia*, religion "which has the effect of nullifying or impairing equality of opportunity or treatment in employment or occupation".[66] It requires each member to "declare and pursue a national policy designed to promote...equality of opportunity and treatment in respect of employment and occupation, with a view to eliminating any discrimination in respect thereof".[67] Each member undertakes to enact legislation in pursuit of this policy[68] and to repeal any statutory provision and modify any administrative instructions or practices which are inconsistent with this policy.[69]

1.37   A more specific declaration on religious discrimination is the 1981 UN General Assembly resolution 36/55. This is a "Declaration on the Elimination of all Forms of Intolerance and of Discrimination Based on Religion or Belief". The Declaration calls upon States to take "effective measures to prevent and eliminate discrimination on the grounds of religion or belief in the recognition, exercise and enjoyment of human rights and fundamental freedoms in all fields of civil, economic, political, social and cultural life".[70]

---

64   ICESCR, art. 2(2).
65   The ILO Convention was ratified on June 8th 1999 and came into force for the UK 12 months later.
66   ILO Convention 111, art. 1(a).
67   Ibid. art. 2.
68   Ibid. art. 3(b).
69   Ibid. art. 3(c).
70   Article 4.

2.

New legislation or amendment to existing legislation?

Q.1   Does the Human Rights Act 1998 provide a sufficient legislative framework for tackling religious discrimination?

2.1   As noted above (paras.1.11 to 1.18) the HRA now provides legal remedies in the UK for religious discrimination in connection with any convention right. This will provide an important avenue for challenging primary and secondary legislation and the acts or omissions of public authorities, where religions or beliefs are treated unequally without objective and reasonable justification. The first question for policy-makers and legislators is whether to allow the limits of the HRA to be tested before embarking on further legislation. The Government will, of course, have to introduce either primary legislation or secondary legislation under the European Communities Act, to implement the EC employment directive. The issue is whether in areas not covered by the directive the HRA provides adequate protection. One *advantage* of the HRA might be thought to be its open-ended nature, enabling the courts to develop religious discrimination law in a sensitive and flexible way in accordance with convention rights. Another advantage, from the viewpoint of the Churches, is that section 13 of the HRA (discussed in para.1.14 above) expressly emphasises that while religious organisations are not exempt, their position is not to be undermined. In any event, any new UK primary legislation would have to take a very broad approach (e.g. on the definition of "religion or belief" discussed in sections 4 and 5 below) so that a declaration of compatibility with convention rights could be made by a Minister under section 19 of the HRA. Any secondary legislation would also have to be drafted so as to be compatible with convention rights.

2.2   There are, however, several *disadvantages* in relying on the HRA on its own. The first is that the courts will have no guidelines from Parliament on a number of difficult and controversial issues, such as the definition of religion or belief and on the limitations which should be imposed on the manifestation of religion or belief. Since these are, in a broad sense, matters of political judgement, it may be thought appropriate that Parliament should deal with them in the first instance. The courts will, of course, still retain the right to scrutinise legislation and the acts and omissions of public authorities so as to ensure that they are compatible with the convention, but this will then be a residuary rather than a primary role. The second disadvantage, as pointed out earlier (para.1.15), is that there is, at present, no free-standing right to complain of religious discrimination. This would be remedied if the Government were to ratify Protocol No.12 (see paras.1.15-17) and the Secretary of State then made an Order under section 1(4) of the HRA to implement it. The third disadvantage is that the HRA applies only to public authorities. Although "public authority" is defined broadly to include "any person whose functions are functions of a public nature", it does not place obligations on private individuals or corporations. Difficult borderline cases will arise where authorities have a mixture of public and private functions as a result of privatisation or local partnership arrangements. A fourth disadvantage is that the scope of Article 14 is problematical so far as the defence of justification of direct discrimination and the concept of indirect discrimination are concerned. These important issues (discussed in sections 6 and 8 below) could be more closely defined in domestic legislation, so creating greater certainty and also consistency with other parts of anti-discrimination law.

Q.2   *Should there be a non-statutory voluntary code on religious discrimination?*

2.3   A second question is whether, instead of specific legislation, the Government should introduce a non-statutory voluntary code of practice on religious discrimination, directed particularly at employers and service providers. In June 1999, a code of this kind was issued by the Government on Age Diversity, and the Government proposes to issue a code in respect of sexual orientation. The Age Diversity Code sets standards against which employers are encouraged to review their practices, and it is supplemented by guidance and case studies to assist employers in carrying out reviews. The implementation of the Code is to be evaluated by 2001, in order to gauge the levels of awareness of the Code among employers and individuals and its effectiveness. The Cabinet Office Performance and Innovation Unit in its report on improving opportunities for people aged 50-65, has recommended that the Government should make it clear that it will introduce age discrimination legislation if the evaluation of the Code of Practice shows it has not been effective.[71]

2.4   The main *advantage* of a code of practice is that it can be relatively easily introduced and updated and avoids imposing bureaucratic requirements on employers and service providers. The main *disadvantage* is that although a voluntary approach may

---

71   Performance and Innovation Unit, Winning the Generation Game (London, HMSO, April 2000), p.60.

succeed in influencing the behaviour of some organisations (e.g. a company whose markets are among various religious communities), it will be disregarded by others who for economic or social reasons are resistant to change. The promise of legislation "at a later date" if voluntary methods fail[72] poses a false dichotomy between voluntary and compulsory methods of regulation. There is, unfortunately, an absence of surveys or case studies as to the attitudes of British employers to legislation on religious discrimination. One must, for the time being therefore turn to evidence from regulatory research in other fields. The general conclusion is that voluntary self-regulation can work only if complemented by measures which are aimed at organisations which fail to comply voluntarily. A comparison may be made in this regard between the Age Diversity Code and the codes issued under the Disability Discrimination Act (DDA). The latter have statutory force and must be taken into account in legal proceedings, as well as being benchmarks for action plans. Case studies of employers, conducted in 1999 for the Independent Review of the Enforcement of UK Anti-Discrimination Legislation indicated that employers generally thought that the voluntary Age Diversity code was ineffective, but praised the codes on disability because of their practical recommendations which were backed by the force of law.[73] A representative survey of 500 members of the Institute of Directors in June 1999 by NOP, showed 63 per cent of employers were in favour of age discrimination legislation,[74] and research among 1700 members of the Institute of Management found 85 per cent of respondents were in favour of comprehensive age discrimination legislation.[75] Small and medium-sized employers are less likely to support legislation, and for this reason legislation needs to be clear and simple and sufficiently flexible to allow account to be taken of the size and administrative resources of those on whom duties are placed.[76]

Q.3   *If new legislation is required, should this be by way of amendment to the Race Relations Act, or by a separate Religious Discrimination Act, or as part of a single Equality Act covering all grounds of unlawful discrimination?*

2.5   If the case for legislation is accepted, how should this be done? **One option** is to cover religious discrimination by amending the RRA. The *advantage* of introducing religious discrimination legislation through an amendment to the RRA,

---

72 As argued by the Better Regulation Task Force, *Review of Anti-Discrimination Legislation,* (London, COI, 1999), p. 4; a view with which the Government agreed in its response (14 July 1999).
73 Hepple, Coussey, Choudhury, *supra n. 1*, para 3.3 and Appendix 1.
74 National Opinion Polls, Survey of 500 IOD members, 1999.
75 Arrowsmith and Goldsmith, *Breaking the Barriers – a survey of managers' attitudes to age and employment* (1996).
76 Hepple, Coussey, Choudhury, *supra n. 1*, esp. para 3.40.

is that it would build upon existing legislation in an evolutionary way rather than requiring new legislation. As noted above, Lord Ahmed recently introduced the Race Relations (Religious Discrimination) Bill which aimed to amend the RRA so as to cover religious discrimination. In his view such an amendment to existing legislation provides the easiest option for reform. He argued that "all that is needed to include religion as an additional ground for proving discrimination by way of differential treatment is to insert the words 'or religious' after the word 'racial' whenever it appears in the wording of the Act, and to insert the word 'or religion' after the word 'race' whenever it appears in the Act".[77]

2.6   The Government has however indicated that amendment of the RRA is not the approach which it favours. It has said that "it is not simply a case of amending the legislation by simply adding religion".[78] The attraction of Lord Ahmed's approach is its apparent simplicity. There are several *disadvantages*. First, religious groups are not usually understood by members of those groups simply as extensions of racial groups. Legislation has an important symbolic function, and the equation of race and religion might send out the wrong signals in a multi-faith society. Secondly, a simple amendment of the kind proposed risks restrictive interpretation by the courts which might regard "religion" as belonging to the same *genus* or category as "race" and "religious group" to the same genus as "racial group". This would exclude from protection members of some religions or religious groups which have no obvious connection with a racial or ethnic group. Finally, it would not be possible to add religion without making specific exemptions relevant to religion which are not at present found in the RRA (see section 8 below).

2.7   If new legislation is to be introduced consideration should also be given to whether it should be an Act dealing with only religious discrimination or whether it should be part of a single Equality Act. The Report of the Independent Review of the Enforcement of UK Anti-Discrimination Legislation has argued that a single Act would recognise the indivisibility of the principle of equality, and encourage links among the groups facing discrimination. It would also make it easier to deal with cases of multiple discrimination, where a person is unfairly treated but does not know the reason.[79] Hybrid situations may arise in which there is discrimination on grounds of ethnic origin combined with discrimination related to religion; just because it is based on one of these grounds does not preclude it from also being based on the other.

---

77   HL Deb, 7 June 2000, c. 1189.
78   *15th UK Periodic Report to the UN Committee on the Elimination of All Forms of Racial Discrimination- Part 1 UK Mainland,* (Home Office Race Equality Unit, 2000), para 229.
79   Hepple, Coussey, Choudhury (2000), *supra* n.1, at para 2.9.

2.8   A new Religious Discrimination Act would provide symbolic value in the recognition of the importance of religious discrimination. However to add a Religious Discrimination Act to the existing legislation may increase the confusion, complexity and inconsistency of anti-discrimination legislation.

3.   Protection for religion/religious belief/ religion or belief?

Q.4   *On what grounds should the legislation prohibit discrimination?*
   - *Religion*
   - *Religious Belief*
   - *Religion or Belief*

Q.5   *Should the legislation cover the lack of all or any religious belief? If so, should this be clearly stated in the legislation?*

3.1   An initial decision, in developing the framework for anti-discrimination legislation, has to be made regarding the prohibited grounds. Should the legislation protect against discrimination on the grounds of "religion" only, or of "religious belief", or should it broaden out to protect against discrimination on the grounds of "religion or belief".

3.2   The **first option** is for the legislation to cover only "religion". Leaving aside, for the moment, the problems that arise in defining religion, it is clear that restricting the legislation to the protection of religion provides relatively greater certainty than the other options. Beliefs are a far broader category than religion. It would be clear, for example, that it does not cover political and ideological beliefs. The restriction of the legislation to religion may exclude from its protection discrimination against those with ethical belief systems which fall outside traditional religions, and might also exclude atheists and agnostics.

3.3   A **second option** would be to prohibit discrimination on the grounds of "religious belief". It can be argued that atheism and agnosticism would be protected by legislation that covers discrimination on the grounds of "religious belief". Even if atheism is not a religion, atheism differs from typical non-religious discourse. The questions atheism and agnosticism deal with concern religion or religious issues. Accordingly the principle of equality would require that they be protected by anti-discrimination legislation in the same way as belief in a religion is treated.[80] Legislation in Britain that prohibited discrimination on the grounds of

---

80   K. Greenwalt, "Diverse Perspectives and the Religion Clause: An Examination of Justification and Qualifying Beliefs", 74(5) *Notre Dame Law Review* 1433 (1999), at p.1463.

religious belief would also ensure consistency with the legislation in Northern Ireland. The definition of religious belief in the FETO includes "the absence...of any, or any particular religious beliefs".[81]

3.4   The **third option,** a broader approach covering both "religion or belief", is consistent with the Article 13 employment directive which refers specifically to prohibiting discrimination in employment on the grounds of, *inter alia*, religion or belief. If the UK legislation were to cover "religion or belief" then the definition of religion would become less of an acute issue. In particular new religious movements would gain the protection of the legislation without the need for their recognition as religions, and it would be clear that non-religious beliefs are covered. (See section 4 below).

3.5   The main problem is that of defining "religion or belief". Neither Article 13 nor the employment directive defines these terms. The House of Lords Select Committee examining the proposal expressed concern that the phrase "would appear to encompass a wide range of political or ideological views" but added "witnesses who commented on this agreed that in practice the courts tended to supply sensible definition of such phrases".[82] They concluded that if protection against discrimination on the grounds of religion or belief is extended beyond the employment field, "a clearer definition, or a list of examples, will be required".[83] The Government acknowledged the Committee's concerns and expects "that it will be left to Members States to define more tightly the phrase "religion or belief" when transposing the Directive. The Government recognises that it will be important to consider the matter of the definition of 'religion or belief' when this takes place".[84] It is to this issue to which we now turn.

---

80   K. Greenwalt, "Diverse Perspectives and the Religion Clause: An Examination of Justification and Qualifying Beliefs", 74(5) Notre Dame Law Review 1433 (1999), at p.1463.
81   FETO, art. 2(3).
82   House of Lords, *supra* n. 49, para 74.
83   House of Lords, *supra* n. 49, para 75.
84   Government Response to Report of the House of Lords Select Committee on the EU Proposals to Combat Discrimination (2000), para 38.

4.

Definition of religion

Q.6   *What should be included as essential elements in any definition of religion?*

4.1   The difficulty of defining religion is regarded as a key obstacle to legislation prohibiting religious discrimination.[85] For those framing legislation there are three options. The **first option** is to attempt a definition within the legislation or through a statutory code of practice. A starting point may be the classical sociological definition of religion set out by Durkheim:

[A] unified system of beliefs and practices relative to sacred things, that is to say, things set apart and forbidden – beliefs and practices which unite into one single moral community called a Church, all those who adhere to them.[86]

Alternatively one could take the Oxford English Dictionary definition of religion as "action or conduct indicating a belief in, reverence for, and desire to please, a divine ruling power; the exercise or practice of rites or observances implying this...a particular system of faith and worship". Lord Ahmed opening a debate on the issue of religious discrimination suggested that religion should be defined as "that system of beliefs and activities centred around the worship of God which is derived in whole or in part from a book revealed by God to one of His messengers".[87] Another broader formulation is that adopted by Ontario Human Rights Commission. The Ontario Human Rights Code prohibits discrimination on the grounds of "creed". Creed is not a defined term in the Code. The Commission's guidance states that:[88]

Creed is interpreted to mean "religious creed" or "religion." It is defined as a professed system and confession of faith, including both beliefs and observances or worship. A belief in a God or gods, or a single Supreme Being or deity is not a pre-requisite. Religion is broadly accepted by the Commission to include, for example, non-deistic bodies of faith, such as the spiritual faiths/practices of aboriginal cultures, as well as bona fide newer religions (assessed on a case by case basis). The existence of religious beliefs and

85   See: HL Deb, 28 October 1999, c. 454-478; Home Office Race Equality Unit, supra n.78, para 229.
86   E. Durkheim, *The Elementary Forms of Religious Life*, 1915, trans. J W Swain, (Free Press, New York, 1975), p. 62.
87   HL Deb, 28 October 1999, c. 457.
88   Ontario Human Rights Commission, *Policy on Creed and the Accommodation of Religious Observances* (1996) available on the Internet at http://www.ohrc.on.ca

practices are both necessary and sufficient to the meaning of creed, if the beliefs and practices are sincerely held and/or observed. "Creed" is defined subjectively. The Code protects personal religious beliefs, practices or observances, even if they are not essential elements of the creed, provided they are sincerely held.

4.2   The advantage of utilising a statutory code of practice, to which the courts must have regard, is that it provides guidance to users of the legislation on where to draw the line while leaving flexibility to deal sensitively with individual cases. However any definition will inevitably exclude some groups and would require further interpretation.

Q.7   *Should there be a list of officially recognised religions? What would be the criteria and the process by which religions gained official recognition?*

4.3   A **second option** is to have a list of recognised religions with a process and criteria for such recognition. The list system is operated to an extent in Germany, where certain religions are given the status of legal person in public law, through procedures in force under Article 140 of the Constitution. The status of legal person gives rise to certain rights, in particular the right to levy church taxes through the services of the State and the right to tax advantages and tax exemptions. A "cult" is granted the status of a legal person in public law when, in light of its statute and its membership, it gives every indication of durability.[89] Recognition requires a "measure of internal organisation, adequate financing, and a certain period of existence; in practice, existence for thirty or forty years is required before a religious community can be considered to have shown sufficient durability."[90] Jehovah's Witnesses and the Church of Scientology and the Muslim Community are among those that have so far not received recognition as legal persons in public law in Germany.

4.4   The creation of lists of accepted religions raises the issue of the recognition of new religious movements. Those who favour an official list system claim a number of advantages. It provides a system of executive supervision to prevent protection being given to fleeting beliefs, or ones which are believed to present a threat to other human rights and values. It also allows for a high degree of certainty as regards the scope of legislation for various purposes. If utilised in the case of anti-discrimination legislation, it would reduce the need for litigation to decide

89   A. Amor, *Implementation of the Declaration on the Elimination of All Forms of Intolerance and Discrimination Based on Religion or Belief* , UN doc E/CN.4/1998/6/Add.2, at para 17.

90   K. Boyle, and J. Sheen, *Freedom of Religion and Belief- A World Report* (London, Routledge, 1997), p. 308.

whether a religious group came within the scope of the Act. There is already some experience of official listing of religions in the UK. The prison chaplaincy service carries out an Annual Religious Census on which Scientologists, Black Muslims and Rastafarians are recorded as "non-permitted religions".[91] The current list of religions used by the Prison Service is set out in Appendix 2.

4.5   The main *disadvantages* of a list system are that it would require an administrative or judicial procedure in order to determine the status of a particular religion. The German system does not exist in the context of an anti-discrimination law, but serves the purpose of conferring a status for purposes such as the right to levy taxes or enjoy privileges. Certainty may be outweighed by rigidity, and the possibly unfair exclusion of new and unpopular beliefs. A law against religious discrimination is primarily concerned with conferring protection on individuals in respect of their own sincerely held beliefs, rather than protecting or legitimating any particular religion.

Q.8   *Is a definition of religion a necessary pre-requisite for legislation to tackle religious discrimination or should this be left for the courts to develop?*

4.6   The **third option** is to leave the definition of religion for the courts to develop. Article 14 of the ECHR prohibits discrimination on the grounds of religion without providing a definition of religion. Most anti-discrimination legislation in Australia, Canada and the United States which prohibits discrimination on the grounds of religion adopts this approach. The definition has been left to the courts, in some cases with guidance provided by the enforcement commission.

4.7   The meaning of "religion" may depend on the purposes of the statute or other legal instrument in which the word is used. Outside the area of discrimination law the legal system does have experience in attempting to define in religion and in establishing principles by which to recognise religions. This shows that no single or universal definition is possible. One context in which the concept is explored is in cases involving charitable trusts set up for the advancement of religion. In re: *South Palace Ethical Society*,[92] Mr. Justice Dillon held that a society for the study and dissemination of ethical principles that did not involve faith in a deity could not constitute religion. He said that:

---

91   S. Poulter, *Ethnicity, Law and Human Rights* (Oxford, Clarendon, 1998), p. 349.
92   *Re South Place Ethical Society Barralet and Others v. Attorney General and others* [1980] 1 WLR 1565.

In a free country…it is natural that the court should desire not to discriminate between beliefs deeply and sincerely held, whether they are beliefs in God or in the excellence of man or in ethical principles or in Platonism or some other scheme of philosophy. But I do not see that that warrants extending the meaning of the word 'religion' so as to embrace all other beliefs and philosophies. Religion, as I see it, is concerned with man's relations with God, and ethics are concerned with man's relations with man. The two are not the same, and are not made the same by sincere inquiry into the question, what is God. If reason leads people not to accept Christianity or any known religion, but they do believe in the excellence of qualities such as truth, beauty and love, or believe in the Platonic concept of the ideal, their beliefs may be to them the equivalent of a religion, but viewed objectively they are not religion…it seems to me that two of the essential attributes of religion are faith and worship; faith in God and worship of that God.[93]

The definition of religion by charitable trusts has been considered more recently by the Charity Commissioners in the light of the HRA. In determining an application by the Church of Scientology the Commissioners reviewed the existing case law and concluded that the "English authorities were neither clear nor unambiguous as to the definition of religion in English Charity law, and at best the cases are of persuasive value with the result that a positive and constructive approach and one which conforms to the ECHR principle, to identifying what is a religion in charity law could and should be adopted".[94] They concluded that while belief in a supreme being was a necessary characteristic of religion for the purposes of English charity law it would not "be proper to specify the nature of that supreme being or to require it to be analogous to the deity or supreme being of a particular religion".[95] The Commissioners concluded that the Church of Scientology did claim to profess a belief in a supreme being.[96] However the Church of Scientology was not recognised as a religion because their core religious service of "auditing and training" was not sufficient for the "reverence and veneration for a supreme being" which the Commissioners considered "necessary to constitute worship in English charity law".[97]

4.8   A second related context is that of taxation. The Australian High Court was unable to reach a consensus on the precise definition of religion when it considered the application of the law on pay-roll taxes.[98] Acting Chief Justice

---

93   Op Cit., at p. 1571.
94   Application for Registration as a charity by the Church of Scientology – Decision of the Charity Commissioners for England and Wales made on the 17th November 1999, at p. 19.
95   Op. Cit., at p. 21.
96   Op. Cit. p.25
97   Op. Cit. p.25
98   Church of the New Faith v. Commissioner for Pay-Roll Tax (Vic) (1983) 154 CLR 120.

Mason and Justice Brennan echoed the narrow approach of the English courts. In their view a religion requires a belief in a supernatural Being, Thing or Principle and the acceptance of canons of conduct to give effect to that belief.[99] Justices Wilson and Deane suggested that there could be no comprehensive definition of religion but held that it was possible to identify characteristics indicating towards the existence of a religion. Justice Murphy took the broadest view; he held that there was "no single acceptable criterion, no essence of religion" and that any organisation which claims to be a religious organisation and which offers a way to find meaning and purpose in life is a religious organisation.[100]

4.9   A third context is that of claims by conscientious objectors for exemption, for example, from military service. US law provides an exemption from military service for persons who by reason of their "religious training and belief are conscientiously opposed to participation of wars of any form".[101] Religious training and belief is defined as "an individual's belief in relation to a 'Supreme Being' involving duties superior to those arising from any human relation, but [not including] essentially political, sociological or philosophical views or a merely personal moral code". The Supreme Court held that the "test of belief 'in a relation to a Supreme Being' is whether a given belief that is sincere and meaningful occupies a place in the life of its possessor parallel to that filled by the orthodox belief in God of one who clearly qualifies for the exemption. Where such beliefs have parallel positions in the lives of their respective holders [the Supreme Court] cannot say that one is 'in a relation to a Supreme Being' and the other is not."[102] In the UK, courts have distinguished the political conscientious objector from the "true" conscientious objector, that is someone who upon religious grounds thinks it is wrong to kill and to resist force.[103]

4.10   Courts and tribunals in the UK had some experience in the 1970s of interpreting "religious belief" and also "conscience" in the context of exemptions from closed shop arrangements. The *Industrial Relations Act 1971*, s.9 granted an exemption to a worker who genuinely objected on grounds of "conscience" to union membership. The National Industrial Relations Court held that, in the context of an individual's reasons for refusing to join a trade union, this "necessarily points to and involves a belief or conviction based on religion in the broadest sense as

99   Op. Cit. 136.
100 Op. Cit. 150.
101 Universal Military Training and Armed Services Act, 50 USC (1958 ed.), s.456(j).
102 *United States v. Seeger* 380 US 163 at 166.
103 *Newell v Gillingham Corporation* [1941] 1 All ER 552, per Atkinson J.

contrasted with personal feeling, however strongly held, or intellectual creed."[104] However, the Employment Appeal Tribunal later disagreed and said that grounds of conscience do not necessarily involve religious belief.[105] The 1971 Act was amended in 1974 so as to limit the exemption to objections to "grounds of religious belief". The Employment Appeal Tribunal held that the belief which falls to be considered is that which is held by the person whose belief is under consideration, rather than an established body of creed or dogma appertaining to the individual as well as a number of other persons.[106]

4.11   It can be seen from this discussion that the third option has the advantage of allowing the courts to interpret "religion" in a way which accords with the purposes of the legislation. The main purpose of anti-discrimination legislation is to protect the individual from arbitrary treatment based on stereotypes or unjustified practices. The courts will not be concerned with the legitimacy of a particular creed, but rather with whether or not there has been discrimination because an individual is believed, rightly or wrongly, to subscribe to those beliefs.

---

104 *Hynds v Spillers-French Baking Ltd* [1974] IRLR 281 at 283, endorsing the views of a tribunal in Drury v The Bakers' Union (Southern District) [1973] IRLR 171.

105 *Saggers v British Railways Board* [1977] IRLR 266 at 267.

106 Ibid. The matter was remitted to the tribunal which again held (by a majority) that, although they accepted the sincerity of the objections of a Jehovah's Witness to membership of a trade union, his objection was on more general grounds of conscience not religious belief. This finding was overturned on appeal as one which no reasonable tribunal could reach on the facts: *Saggers v British Railways Board (No.2)* [1978] IRLR 435.

5.   Definition of belief

Q.9.   What should be included as essential elements in any definition of belief?

Q.10.   Is a definition of belief a necessary pre-requisite for legislation to tackle discrimination on the grounds of religion or belief or should this be left for the courts to develop?

5.1   No one argues that there should be an official list of recognised beliefs. But is some definition necessary? The House of Lords Select Committee looking at the Article 13 draft employment directive expressed concern that belief "would appear to encompass a wide range of political or ideological views". The issues and options raised by the definition of 'belief' are similar to those surrounding the definition of religion.

5.2   Again, the **first option** would be to provide a definition in the legislation or a statutory code of practice. The **second option** would be to leave this to the courts. The ECHR may be of some assistance here. The broad approach of the Convention organs to the interpretation of Article 9 has enabled them to accept, in principle, that its protection extends to Druidism,[107] pacifism,[108] veganism,[109] the Divine Light Zentrum[110] and the Church of Scientology.[111] The European Court of Human Rights has said that Article 9 is a "precious asset for atheists, agnostics, sceptics and the unconcerned".[112] This does not, however, mean that every individual opinion or preference constitutes a religion or belief. To come within the protection of this article the views must attain a certain level of cogency, seriousness, cohesion and importance.[113] In McFeely v UK the Commission said that "belief" in Article 9 "means more than just 'mere opinions or deeply held feelings'; there must be a holding of spiritual or philosophical convictions which have an identifiable formal content".[114] The courts may in future be guided, when interpreting the Article 13 employment directive, by the EU Charter of

---

107 *Chappell v UK* (1987) 53 DR 241.
108 *Arrowsmith v UK* (1978) 19 DR 5.
109 *X v UK* (Commission) Appl 18187/91 (10 February 1993).
110 *Omkarananda and the Divine Light Zentrum v Switzerland* (1981) 25 DR 105.
111 *X and Church of Scientology v Sweden* (1979) 16 DR 68.
112 *Kokkinakis v Greece* (1994) 17 EHRR 397 at para 31.
113 *Campbell and Cosans v UK* (1982) 4 EHRR 293.
114 [1981] 3 EHRR 161.

Fundamental Rights, Article 1 of which says that "the dignity of the person must be respected and protected". Those beliefs which are essential to the dignity and integrity of the individual are likely to be protected as an aspect of freedom of belief. On the other hand, the courts may be unwilling to allow political or ideological views (e.g. against the criminalisation of drugs or against genetically modified foods) to qualify as a "belief".

5.3   The UN Human Rights Committee has also recognised that the definition of "religion or belief" should be subjected to certain limits. In the case of *M.A.B.; W.A.T. and A.Y.T. v Canada*[115] the applicants argued that the Canadian *Narcotics Control Act* violated their right to freedom of thought, conscience and religion under Article 18 of the ICCPR because it prohibited the use of marijuana. The applicants were associated with the Assembly of the Church of the Universe. Their beliefs and practices included the care, cultivation, possession, distribution, maintenance, integrity and worship of marijuana, which they referred to as the "sacrament" of the Church. The Committee said that the expression "religion or belief" does not encompass a belief which consists primarily or exclusively of the worship of and distribution of a narcotic drug.[116] A further safeguard is provided by Article 9(2) of the ECHR which allows for limitations on the manifestation of beliefs to be prescribed by law provided that the test of necessity is met (see para.1.12). This would mean that although an employee could not be dismissed simply for holding extreme beliefs, dismissal or other discriminatory treatment for the manifestation of those beliefs, for example by proselytising other employees or engaging in disruptive behaviour, could be justified if this could be shown to be necessary for the protection of public order or health or morals or to protect "the rights and freedoms of others."

---

115 Communication No. 570/1993, Inadmissibility Decision of April 8 1994, cited in *Article 18- Freedom of Religion and Belief,* (Human Rights and Equal Opportunities Commission, 1998), at p. 11.

116 Even where the religion or belief is protected, religious observances (such as the use of prohibited drugs) may be restricted if this is objectively justified and reasonable (e.g. because of the harm caused by drugs): see *Price v President of the Law Society of the Cape of Good Hope 1998* (8) Butterworths Constitutional Law Reports 976 (C).

6.   Definition of discrimination

6.1   Current UK law provides two separate models for the definition of discrimination. The **first model**, found in the UK's race and sex discrimination legislation, and in Northern Ireland's fair employment legislation, prohibits both direct and indirect discrimination. Direct discrimination is permissible only if it falls within certain specific exemptions, such as genuine occupational qualifications. Under this approach there is no general justification for direct discrimination. There is however a general defence of justification for indirect discrimination. The *Disability Discrimination Act* 1995 (DDA) provides a **second model** for framing anti-discrimination legislation. The DDA prohibits discrimination for a reason related to a person's disability. It defines discrimination in two ways: (1) direct discrimination, and (2) failure to comply with the duty to make reasonable adjustments for a disabled person. Both are subject to a general defence of justification. The DDA does not cover indirect discrimination as such. A **third model** is found in the provisions of the Article 13 employment directive relating to disability and in Canadian legislation relating to religious discrimination. These seek to combine the duty to make adjustments within the definition of indirect discrimination. In developing legislation to cover religious discrimination one must decide which legislative model would be most effective. This section examines each of these options.

(A) Direct and indirect discrimination

Q.11   *Should the legislation prohibit (a) direct discrimination, (b) indirect discrimination and (c) harassment?*

Q.12   *What should be the definition of indirect discrimination?*

6.2   The first model is that found in the RRA, SDA and FETO. This prohibits both direct and indirect discrimination. By extension this is interpreted to include harassment. The Article 13 employment directive specifically deems harassment to be a form of discrimination. Direct discrimination is defined as treating a person of the protected group less favourably than others not of that group are or would be treated. Any legislation on religious discrimination must undoubtedly include this principle of formal equality or consistent treatment, since this is the starting-point of any anti-discrimination measure. However, its limitations must be understood. The principle of consistent treatment is satisfied regardless of whether the complainant benefits as a result. For example if an employer refused to allow a Muslim time off for prayers, or refused to allow a Muslim woman to wear a headscarf this could only amount to direct discrimination on grounds of religion if non-Muslim employees were allowed such rights. (The female might have a claim of direct sex discrimination if male employees were not subject to a dress code, but this would not be on grounds of religion.) Direct discrimination requires a comparator whose relevant circumstances are the same or not materially different from those of the complainant. The principle can be satisfied by treating members of the compared groups equally badly (levelling down) as well as by conferring benefits on them both (levelling up). Generally speaking there can be direct discrimination without any conscious motivation on the part of the discriminator.[117] The question is essentially one of causation. Applied to religious discrimination this would be: but for the person's religion or belief would that person have been differently treated? Religion or belief would need to be the activating cause and so it seems that the discriminator would need to have knowledge or a belief as to the person's religion or belief.[118]

6.3   The concept of indirect discrimination was developed in the USA by way of case law under Title VII of the *Civil Rights Act 1964* (which includes in its coverage discrimination on grounds of religion or creed). This was adapted into the statutory concept found in the SDA, RRA and FETO. The concept has been developed by case law of the European Court of Justice (in respect of sex and nationality) and also by the UK courts. There are now no less than three different statutory definitions. The first is that in the RRA, SDA and FETO. The second is that relating to sex discrimination only in the EC Burden of Proof Directive. The third is in the Article 13 EC employment directive, and in the race directive. Legislation on religious discrimination would have to choose between these three models.

6.4   The **first option** is the definition in the RRA. It must be shown (1) that a "requirement or condition" was applied to a person which applies or would apply equally to persons not of the same racial group as that person; (2) the requirement or condition is such that the proportion of persons of the same racial group as that

---

117   *Nagarajan v London Regional Transport* [1999] ICR 877, House of Lords.
118   *Seide v Gillette Industries* Ltd [1980] IRLR 427 at 431. If the DDA model (below) were followed, however, with a defence of justification to direct discrimination, then it may be argued that such knowledge is not essential; this is a disputed point, however: compare *H.J.Heinz Co v Kenrick* [2000] IRLR 144, with *O'Neill v Symm & Co. Ltd.* [1998] IRLR 233.

person who can comply is considerably smaller than the proportion of persons not of that racial group who can comply with it; (3) the respondent cannot show that it is justifiable irrespective of the colour, race, nationality or ethnic or national origins of the person to whom it is applied; and (4) it is to the detriment of that person because he or she cannot comply with it. A similar definition is found in FETO, with "religious group" and "religion or political opinion" instead of "racial group" and "colour, race etc."[119] One difficulty with this definition is that it has been judicially decided that a "requirement or condition" must be an absolute bar to compliance.[120] In the Perera case, an applicant for the post of legal assistant in the civil service had to be either a qualified solicitor or barrister and had to receive a satisfactory assessment from the interviewing board. Among the factors that the interviewing board took into consideration in making its assessment was experience in the UK, and Mr Perera, who was born in Sri Lanka and had been in the UK for 7 years, claimed that this was indirectly discriminatory on grounds of national origin. The Court of Appeal held consideration of this factor did not constitute a "requirement or condition" because it was not an absolute bar to selection. Candidates who performed poorly in relation to one of the factors could compensate by doing well in relation to another of the factors. Thus no one factor constituted an absolute bar and so there could be no requirement or condition. The SDA is similarly worded, but in the context of sex discrimination, the European Court of Justice has indicated that all that need be shown is a "provision, criterion, policy or practice" and that this need not be an absolute bar.[121] This has not, however, yet been translated into the domestic law on racial discrimination. This will have to be changed to comply with the race directive (below). It would be out of step with that and other developments (below) for the RRA and FETO definitions to be copied in religious discrimination legislation.

6.5   A **second option** is to be found in Article 2(2) of the Burden of Proof Directive 97/80/EC which codifies the case law of the European Court of Justice on sex discrimination. It reads:

> For the purposes of the principle of equal treatment...indirect discrimination shall exist where an apparently neutral provision, criterion or practice disadvantages a substantially higher proportion of the members of one sex unless that provision, criterion or practice is appropriate and necessary and can be justified by objective factors unrelated to sex.

---

119 RRA s. 1(1)(b); RR(NI)O, art. 3(1)(b); FETO, art. 3(2)(b). To same effect are SDA, s. 1(1)(b); SD(NI)O, art.3(1)(b).

120 *Perera v. Civil Service Commission (2) and Department of Customs and Excise* [1983] IRLR 166 CA.

121 Case C-127/92, *Enderby v Frenchay Health Authority* [1993] ICR 591; cf *Bhudi v IMI Refineries Ltd* [1994] IRLR 204.

This formulation overcomes the need to show a "requirement or condition" (above para 6.4), and it also clarifies the test of proportionality which must be applied when establishing objective justification. It sets out the test of a substantially higher proportion who can comply for making the relevant comparison. This is the formulation favoured by the Independent Review of UK Anti-Discrimination Legislation.[122] The Government proposes to implement this definition in sex discrimination legislation in respect of employment and vocational training.[123]

6.6   A **third option** is the definition in Article 2(2)(b) of the Article 13 employment directive, which reads:

Indirect discrimination shall be taken to occur where an apparently neutral provision, criterion or practice would put persons having a particular religion or belief, a particular disability, a particular age, or a particular sexual orientation at a particular disadvantage compared with other persons, unless:

(i)   that provision, criterion or practice is objectively justified by a legitimate aim and the means of achieving it are appropriate and necessary...

This is similar to the definition in the race directive which refers to putting "persons of a racial or ethnic origin at a particular disadvantage". These definitions of indirect discrimination differ from that in the Burden of Proof Directive is three ways. Firstly, they do not require a complainant to demonstrate that a given practice has in fact had an adverse effect. It is sufficient that it "would" have such an effect. The European Commission has argued that this formulation removes the need to demonstrate statistically that indirect discrimination has occurred.[124] Secondly, the definition in the employment directive refers to indirect discrimination occurring where a provision, criterion or practice puts "persons having a particular religion or belief" at a particular disadvantage. The US case law from which this concept derives, as well as the settled case law of the ECJ in relation to nationality and sex discrimination, as codified in article 2(2) of the Burden of Proof Directive (above), makes it clear that the effect must be on members of a group, not simply individuals. The employment directive does not make it clear that the disadvantage must be suffered by a group of persons of a particular religion or belief to which the complainant adheres in comparison with persons not of that group. Literally interpreted, there will be indirect discrimination if two or more persons of a

122   Hepple, Coussey and Choudhury, *supra* n. 1, at para 2.31.
123   DfEE, *Towards Equal Pay for Women*, Consultation Paper (December 2000).
124   House of Lords, *supra* n. 49, at para 80.

particular religion or belief suffer a particular disadvantage even without evidence that the members generally of the religious group suffer disadvantage.[125] Thirdly, the employment directive measures disparate impact by requiring a "particular disadvantage". This was justified by the European Commission on the ground that it was "extremely complicated" to develop statistical assessments. Indeed, in some Member States ethnic monitoring does not take place, and monitoring of religious affiliation may also be rare.

6.7   The notion of a "considerably smaller" proportion of a group being able to comply has been flexibly interpreted by the UK courts and tribunals so as to permit judicial notice to be taken of social facts without the need for elaborate statistical evidence.[126] Accordingly, it is questionable whether the concept of "particular disadvantage" adds anything of substance to UK law. Putting persons at a "particular disadvantage" seems to be no different from the "less favourable treatment" covered by the notion of direct discrimination. Indirect discrimination is concerned with the disproportionate impact of a criterion or practice on a particular group, defined by race, religion, sex etc. In the view of the House of Lords Select Committee these different definitions of indirect discrimination "can only create confusion and increase the burden of litigation on the courts and employers."[127] An overriding consideration, in the interests of simplicity, may be to adopt the same definition in respect of all grounds of unlawful discrimination, including religion.

(B) Indirect discrimination and reasonable accommodation

Q.13   Should indirect discrimination be combined with a duty to make reasonable adjustments?

6.8   Introducing the idea of reasonable adjustment or accommodation signifies an important shift in the understanding of equality. In the DDA the concept of indirect discrimination is not used but there is a primary duty to make reasonable adjustments where arrangements or physical features of premises place a disabled person at a substantial disadvantage compared with persons who are not disabled. In Northern Ireland, in the case of discrimination on grounds of religion or political opinion, the duty to promote equality of opportunity includes affirmative action

---

125   Ibid.
126   See e.g. *London Underground Ltd v Edwards* (No.2) [1998] IRLR 364.
127   House of Lords, *supra* n. 49, at para 84.

defined in terms of steps to increase fair participation and fair access (para.1.5 above). In the context of religious discrimination in Britain it is argued that there is a need to accommodate diversity because our society is already structured around basic Christian assumptions and therefore already accommodates the needs of Christians, for example Christmas and Easter are recognised as public holidays, and shop workers and betting workers have the right to object to Sunday working.[128] In a multi-faith multi-cultural society, the needs of individuals with different religious faiths should be met. This was something understood by Lord Scarman in 1978 when, in a case involving a dispute between a Muslim teacher who requested time to attend Friday prayers and the local education authority, he argued that "room has to be found for teachers and pupils of the new religions in the educational system, if discrimination is to be avoided. This calls not for a policy of the blind eye but for one of understanding. The system must be made flexible to accommodate their beliefs and their observances. Otherwise they will suffer discrimination".[129] Justice McIntyre in the Canadian Supreme Court also recognised that "the accommodation of differences...is the essence of true equality".[130] Others have pointed towards the dangers of reasonable accommodation. Lord Denning in *Ahmad* took the view that it would do a minority group "no good, if they were to be given preferential treatment over the great majority of people. If it should happen that, in the name of religious freedom, they were given special privileges or advantages, it would provoke discontent, and even resentment among those with whom they work...and so the cause of racial integration would suffer. So, whilst upholding religious freedom to the full, I would suggest that it should be applied with caution, especially having regard to the setting in which it is sought".[131] Lord Justice Orr also objected to pursuing a policy of reasonable accommodation. He argued that this would lead to "resentment among non-Moslem staff at having to assume additional burdens and possibly to a situation in which education authorities would have been reluctant to employ more Moslem teachers".[132] More recently, Gay Moon and Robin Allen QC have argued that "too great an emphasis on an obligation to make adjustments could lead to a more restrictive interpretation of religion or belief. This might cause the adjustments necessary for a fundamental right to be inappropriately limited in practice."[133]

---

128 Employment Rights Act 1996, Part IV.
129 *Ahmad v Inner London Education Authority* [1978] 1 All ER 574 at 583.
130 Andrews v. Law Society of British Columbia 10 C.H.R.R. D/5719 at D/5742.
131 *Ahmad v Inner London Education Authority* [1978] 1 All ER 574 at 577-578.
132 Op. Cit. at 581.
133 Gay Moon and Robin Allen QC, "Substantive Rights and Equal Treatment in Respect of Religion and Belief: Towards a Better Understanding of the Rights and their Implications", [2000] *European Human Rights Law Review* 580 at 601.

6.9   There are several *disadvantages* to the approach in the DDA of not utilising the concept of indirect discrimination. The issues in DDA cases revolve initially around whether or not the employer knew that the disabled person needed a reasonable adjustment. This does not arise with indirect discrimination. There the question is whether or not the apparently neutral provision, criterion or practice can be shown to have an adverse impact on a particular group, and if it does, whether the provision is objectively justifiable. The reasonable adjustment approach therefore places the onus on the individual to disclose a disability and explain that the arrangements place him or her at a substantial disadvantage. If he or she succeeds in doing this the result will be an individualised solution. The next disabled person will have to go though the same process of disclosure and negotiating reasonableness. The indirect discrimination approach, on the other hand, requires "equality proofing". The onus on the employer or service provider to consider in advance whether or not a provision or practice indirectly discriminates and, if so, whether it is objectively justifiable. The indirect discrimination approach is easier for the individual and can have a much more significant impact in terms of promoting participation and access by the disadvantaged group. The absence of a concept of indirect discrimination in the DDA means that until a disabled person interacts with an employer or service provider, there is no incentive to make adjustments. Moreover, it is by no means clear that all the situations covered by indirect discrimination will be covered by duty to make reasonable adjustments.

6.10   The Article 13 employment directive prohibits both direct and indirect discrimination on all the grounds it covers including disability. It then has a separate Article 5 covering disability:

> In order to guarantee compliance with the principle of equal treatment in relation to persons with disabilities, reasonable accommodation shall be provided. This means that employers shall take appropriate measures, where needed in a particular case, to enable a person with a disability to have access to, participate in, or advance in employment, or to undergo training, unless such measures would impose a disproportionate burden on the employer. The burden shall not be disproportionate when it is sufficiently remedied by measures existing within the framework of the disability policy of the Member State concerned.

Thus the directive applies the concept of indirect discrimination as well as reasonable accommodation, but only in respect of disability. The House of Lords Committee examining the draft directive noted in their report that "witnesses were divided on the desirability of applying both these concepts". The Committee was "not convinced that applying the concept of indirect discrimination to disability will reinforce the protection already afforded by the DDA's imposition of a duty to provide 'reasonable adjustments'...The drafting of the proposed directive is at present unsatisfactory...[I]f the two concepts are combined then the relationship between them [needs to be] clarified".[134] The Government agreed that the relationship was unclear in the draft directive and needed to be clarified. It also argued that "the concept of 'reasonable adjustment' already provides protection for disabled people in circumstances where the concept of 'indirect discrimination' might otherwise be expected to help".[135] This point was met in the final version of Article 2(2)(b) of the employment directive which now provides an exception to the definition of indirect discrimination (above). Indirect discrimination does not occur:

> As regards persons with a particular disability [where] the employer or any person or organisation to whom this Directive applies, is obliged, under national legislation, to take appropriate measures in line with the principles contained in Article 5 in order to eliminate disadvantages entailed by such provision, criterion or practice.

6.11   The *Ontario Human Rights Code* has also attempted to combine the concept of reasonable adjustment within the concept of indirect discrimination. It goes further than the Article 13 employment directive by applying this to religious discrimination. The Code introduces the concept of "constructive discrimination" which is similar to indirect discrimination. Section 11 of the Code provides a defence to claims of constructive discrimination where "the requirement, qualification or factor is reasonable and bona fide in the circumstances". The provision goes on to state that "a court shall not find that a requirement, qualification or factor is reasonable and bona fide in the circumstances unless it is satisfied that the needs of the group of which the person is a member **cannot be accommodated without undue hardship** on the person responsible for accommodating those needs, considering the cost, outside sources of funding, if any, and health and safety requirements, if any."[136] This formulation has the advantage of clarifying the relationship between indirect discrimination and the duty to make reasonable adjustments. The Independent Review of the Enforcement of UK Anti-Discrimination Legislation proposed that this approach should be adopted in the UK.[137]

---

134   House of Lords, *supra* n. 49, at para 95.
135   Government Response to House of Lords Report, para 51.
136   R.S.O. 1990, c. H.19, s. 11(2).
137   Hepple, Coussey, Choudhury, *supra* n. 1, para 2.33.

7.

The areas covered

Q.14 *What areas of activity should be covered by legislation on religious discrimination?*

7.1 **One option** would be to limit legislation to the areas covered by the Article 13 employment directive. These are –

(a) conditions for access to employment, to self-employment or to occupation, including selection criteria and recruitment conditions, whatever the branch of activity and at all levels of the professional hierarchy including promotion;

(b) access to all types and to all levels of vocational guidance, vocational training, advanced vocational training, and retraining, including practical work experience;

(c) employment and working conditions, including dismissals and pay;

(d) membership of, and involvement in, an organisation of workers or employers, or any organisation whose members carry on a particular profession, including the benefits provided for by such organisations.

Unlike the race directive the employment directive does not apply to payments of any kind made by state schemes or similar, including state social security or social protection schemes. Nor does it apply to the provision of goods, facilities or services, housing, health services and education. If UK religious discrimination legislation were limited to the areas covered by the directive, complaints of religious discrimination by public authorities in other areas such as education, health care, policing, immigration and housing could still be dealt with under the HRA. The main *disadvantage* of this option is that protection under Article 14 of the ECHR is limited to discrimination in respect of convention rights (para.1.16 above). If the Government were to sign, ratify and implement Protocol No.12 there would be a remedy against public authorities for religious discrimination in respect of any legal right.

7.2 A **second option** would be to go beyond the employment directive, and to cover all the areas covered by the RRA as amended. In Northern Ireland the fair employment legislation was extended in 1998 to cover the provision of goods and services. The *advantage* of such an extension is the consistent treatment of racial and religious discrimination, which may be interlinked. A *disadvantage* is that complex exceptions would be necessary to deal in certain areas with the special needs of religious groups as well as the constitutional position of the Established Church.

Q.15   *Should legislation prohibiting religious discrimination cover all public authorities, including schools and education authorities?*

7.3   As a result of the *Race Relations (Amendment) Act 2000* the RRA now covers discrimination by virtually all public authorities. The Article 13 employment directive applies to all persons, both in the public and private sectors including public bodies. This appears to include the armed forces, who are exempted by the employment directive only in respect of age and disability discrimination.

7.4   The most controversial and difficult area is that of education. The UK has religious schools both in the state and independent sector. Both the SDA and RRA include discrimination in education within the prohibition of discrimination on the grounds of goods, service and facilities, although there are special procedures for enforcement. Consideration is given in the next section to the exemptions that may be needed for employment in religious schools and organisations.

8.   Exemptions allowing discrimination

8.1   Most jobs require employees to have certain skills or qualifications in order to undertake the work competently and safely. It is not discrimination if a person does not get a job because he or she does not have these skills. The basic premise of anti-discrimination legislation is that employers are under an obligation to consider each applicant on his or her merits in light of these inherent requirements rather than making judgements on the basis of arbitrary factors such as religion or belief. In some employment situations, the question arises as to whether belonging to a specific faith is an inherent requirement of the job. The most obvious example is a minister of religion.

8.2   Several issues relating to exemptions require consideration. *Firstly*, should there be a general defence of justification to a claim of direct discrimination or should the legislation permit only specific exemptions. *Secondly*, if religious discrimination is only allowed where there is a specific exemption in the employment context, should this be worded in broad terms or should specific jobs be identified for which discrimination on the grounds of religion is permitted. *Thirdly*, should there be an exemption for religious bodies that allows them to discriminate on other prohibited grounds where such discrimination is required in order to follow the tenets of their faith. *Finally*, what exemptions are needed in relation to the provision of goods, services and facilities?

Q.16   *Should there be a general defence of justification for direct discrimination or should there be only specific exemptions?*

8.3   Under the RRA and SDA (and in Northern Ireland FETO) direct discrimination is unlawful unless it is covered by one of the specific legislative exemptions (e.g. genuine occupational qualification, positive action, pregnancy and confinement benefits). By contrast the two forms of disability discrimination in DDA s.5 are subject to a much more general defence of objective justification. Under the ECHR, the European Court of Human Rights has also accepted a general defence of justification:

> A difference of treatment is discriminatory if it has no objective and reasonable justification, that is, if it does not pursue a legitimate aim or if there is not a reasonable relationship of proportionality between the means employed and the aims to be realised.[138]

---

138 *Abdulaziz, Cabales and Balkandali v UK* [1985] 7 EHRR 471.

The new Protocol No. 12 to the ECHR makes no reference to justification, apparently on the grounds that justifiable distinctions are not discriminatory in the first place (see above para.1.16). The advantage of a general justification defence is that it allows courts to respond flexibly to situations that were not considered at the time of drafting the exemptions. The disadvantage is that such a defence may create confusion and uncertainty and undermine the principle of equality. Employers and others in a position to discriminate would not know their position, in the absence of earlier case law on the same issue, until the matter has been litigated.

Q.17   *If there are to be specific exemptions should they be worded in broad terms, and if so what should the formulation be? For example, should there be an exemption where belonging to a particular faith is a genuine occupational qualification or requirement?*

8.4   If there are to be specific exemptions allowing direct discrimination rather than a general defence to such discrimination, there are two options for framing the legislative provisions. The **first option** is to have a generally worded exemption. This is the approach taken by the Article 13 employment directive and in article 70 of FETO. Article 4(1) of the directive states:

(1)... Member States may provide that a difference of treatment which is based on a characteristic related to any of the discriminatory grounds referred to in Article 1 [this includes religion or belief] shall not constitute discrimination where, by reason of the nature of the particular occupational activities concerned or of the context in which they are carried out, such a characteristic constitutes a genuine and determining occupational qualification, provided that the objective is legitimate and the requirement is proportionate.

The proposals in an earlier draft of article 4(1) were found by the House of Lords Select Committee to provide "sufficient safeguards for religious organisations."[139]

8.5   Northern Ireland's fair employment legislation provides an exemption for "any employment or occupation where the essential nature of the job requires it to be done by a person holding, or not holding, a particular religious belief".[140] The wording in FETO may be considered clearer than that in the directive.[141] The reference to "the essential nature of the job" makes it clear where adherence to or propagation of the faith is not required – for example cleaners and service staff and teachers in certain subjects – the exemption would not apply.

---

139 House of Lords, *supra* n. 49, at para 111.
140 FETO, art. 70.
141 Hepple, Coussey, Choudhury, *supra* n. 1, para 2.46

8.6   In the Manitoba Human Rights Code the exemption is formulated in terms of the discrimination being reasonable and a "bona fide occupational qualification or requirement".[142] The Supreme Court of Canada in the case of *Ontario Human Rights Commission v. Etobicoke*[143] gave consideration to what constitutes a bona fide and reasonable requirement. It held that "to be a bona fide occupational qualification and requirement a limitation...must be imposed honestly, in good faith, and in the sincerely held belief that such limitation is imposed in the interests of the adequate performance of the work involved with all reasonable dispatch, safety and economy, and not for ulterior and extraneous reasons aimed at objectives which could defeat the purpose of the Code".[144]

Q.18   *Alternatively, should there be a list of specific posts that are exempt from legislation prohibiting religious discrimination? If so, what posts would be included in that list?*

8.7   The **second option** is to identify specific exemptions. This is the approach in the RRA and SDA. Both provide for a number of "genuine occupational qualifications" under which an otherwise discriminatory act would not be unlawful. The RRA grants an exemption where, for reasons of authenticity, dramatic performances require a person of a particular racial group, as also for artistic or photographic modelling, and employment in an ethnic restaurant.[145] Specific exemptions are provided for by the *New Zealand Human Rights Act* 1993:

        28(2) Nothing in s 22 of this Act shall prevent different treatment based on religious or ethical belief where...(b) The sole or principle duties of the position (i) Are or are substantially the same as those of a clergyman, priest, pastor, official, or teacher among the adherents of that belief or otherwise involve the propagation of that belief; or (ii) Are those of a teacher in a private school or (iii) Consist of acting as a social worker on behalf of an organisation whose members consist solely or principally adherents of that belief.

8.8   The Association of Muslim Lawyers (AML) has suggested that exceptions, in relation to Islam, be allowed for the appointment of Directors to Islamic Centres, Imams in mosques and certain teachers in Muslim schools. This could be met by specific exemptions, but it might be more appropriate to deal with this by way of general exemption, as in FETO. The *advantage* of specific exempted posts is

---

142   s. 14(1).
143   [1982] 1 SCR 202
144   [1982] 1 SCR 202, p. 208.
145   RRA, s. 5(2).

certainty. The *disadvantage* is that specific exemptions are inflexible and cannot easily be changed as new situations arise. Another specific exemption suggested by the AML relates to anyone employed in the UK but required to work in places where only Muslims are permitted, such as Mecca and Medina in Saudi Arabia.[146] For the avoidance of doubt, this could be dealt with by a specific exemption.

Q. 19   *Should there be a general exemption that allows particular persons or bodies to discriminate in employment where it is necessary to do so in order to comply with the organisation's religious ethos?*

Q. 20   *To whom should this exemption apply?*

8.9   Concern was expressed during the debate on the report of the House of Lords Committee on the EU proposals that the provision relating to genuine occupational requirements (above) would not provide a sufficient exemption for religious organisations.[147] In response to this the Government said that they would "press for amendments to the directive to ensure that there is no question of religious organisations being forced to employ people who are not members of the relevant faith".[148] Article 4(2) was substantially amended before adoption of the directive to provide that:

Member States may maintain national legislation in force at the date of the adoption of this Directive or provide for future legislation incorporating national practices existing at the date of the adoption of this Directive pursuant to which, in the case of occupational activities within churches and other public or private organisations the ethos of which is based on religion or belief, a difference of treatment based on a person's religion or belief shall not constitute discrimination where, by reason of the nature of these activities or of the context in which they are carried out, a person's religion or belief constitute a genuine, legitimate and justified occupational requirement, having regard to the organisation's ethos. This difference of treatment shall be implemented taking account of Member States' constitutional provisions and principles, as well as the general principles of Community law, and should not justify discrimination on another ground.

146   The Association of Muslim Lawyers, *Religious Discrimination and the Law – Paper for the Commission on British Muslims – Seminar on Religious Discrimination,* (December 1999), at p. 5.
147   HL Deb, 30 June 2000, c.1186.
148   HL Deb, 30 June 2000, c. 1238.

Provided that its provisions are otherwise complied with, this Directive shall thus not prejudice the right of churches and other public or private organisations, the ethos of which is based on religion or belief, acting in conformity with national constitutions and laws, to require individuals working for them to act in good faith and in accordance with the organisation's ethos.

8.10   The first point to note about this complex exemption is that it is permissive. Member States may take advantage of it but need not do so. Secondly, it can be used only to maintain existing legislation or to legislate in respect of existing national practices. It cannot be used to create some new religious restriction. Thirdly, it may be applied not only to churches but also to "other public or private organisations the ethos of which is based on religion or belief". In this respect it would be open to the UK either to use this general wording or to specify the organisations to which it applied. The general wording carries the disadvantage that the exemption may be abused. If an employer could decline to employ Muslims or Jews on the basis that the "ethos" of the business is Christian, this would subvert the whole purpose of a prohibition on discrimination. If the exemption is to be limited then it will be important to clarify which organisations are allowed to discriminate. The Australian *Human Rights and Equal Opportunities Commission Act 1986* provides an exemption for "an institution that is conducted in accordance with the doctrines, tenets, beliefs, teachings of a particular religion or creed". It permits such institutions to make, in good faith, a distinction, exclusion or preference which is necessary "to avoid injury to the religious susceptibilities of adherents of that religion or that creed".[149] The exemption does not apply to any organisation simply on the basis that the organisation or persons associated with it have certain religious views or affiliations.[150] It would most clearly apply to bodies that carry out religious activities, bodies that are, for example, responsible for organising worship, preaching, religious instruction and ceremonial activities. But to what extent should it cover religious organisations that provide services of a more secular nature, such as religious charities, schools and hospices? (The issue of religious schools is discussed below). **One option**, which seems to be in accordance with the purposes of the directive, is to limit the protected organisations to charitable bodies whose principal purpose is the promotion of a particular religion or belief.

---

149 s.3(1)(d).
150 *Guidelines on religious criteria in employment for organisations that provide community services on behalf of the Commonwealth*, (Human Rights and Equal Opportunity Commission, 2000), at p. 6.

8.11   Fourthly, the directive requires that the person's religion or belief must be a genuine, legitimate and justified occupational requirement having regard to the organisation's ethos. This seems to be no more than a repetition, in the specific context of religion and belief, of the general exemption in Article 4(1) (above para 8.4).

8.12   The final paragraph of Article 4(2) deals with the separate point of the duty of loyalty. An example might be a doctor employed in a Catholic hospital who expressed views contrary to those of the Church on the subject of abortion. Any restriction on such an employee's freedom of expression is now subject to Article 10 of the ECHR. The employer would have to justify any restriction, demonstrating a reasonable relationship between that restriction and the nature of the employment and the importance of the issue to the ethos of the organisation. A further restriction is that if the employee is a whistleblower, he or she may be protected under the *Public Interest Disclosure Act 1998*.

Q. 21   *Should there be an exemption allowing discrimination by religious bodies in the provision of goods, services, facilities and education?*

8.13   So far the discussion has centred on exemption to discrimination in employment. If the legislation is extended to the provision of goods, services and facilities other exemptions will be needed. The exact exemptions depend on the areas that are covered. FETO contains an exemption for "goods, facilities or services provided by, or on behalf of, a religious denomination where the essential nature of the goods, facilities or services requires them to be provided only to persons holding or not holding a particular religious belief".[151] Legislation in other jurisdictions also provides some guidance. Ireland's *Equal Status Act 2000* contains exemptions allowing discrimination on the grounds of religion for the provision of goods and services provided for a religious purpose.[152]

8.14   The use of land or buildings for religious purposes is another area where exemptions are often thought to be necessary. In Ireland, there are exemptions in relation to the disposal of premises and the provision of accommodation where "any premises or accommodation are reserved for the use of persons in a particular category of persons for a religious purpose".[153] The Queensland *Anti-Discrimination Act 1991* contains exemptions allowing for discrimination in relation to access to a

151   FETO, art 31(3).
152   ESA, s. 5(2)(e).
153   ESA, s. 6(5).

land or a building of a cultural or religious significance by people who are not of a particular sex, age, or religion where the restriction is in accordance with the culture concerned or the doctrine of the religion concerned and is necessary to avoid offending the cultural or religious sensitivities of people of the culture or religion.[154] It contains similar exemptions for the disposition of land where the relevant interest in land is an interest in land or a building of cultural or religious significance;[155] or in relation to accommodation where the accommodation concerned is under the direction or control of a body established for religious purposes.[156]

8.15   There is an exemption in the Republic of Ireland legislation allowing discrimination in the membership of clubs where the principal purpose of the club is to meet the needs of persons of a particular religious belief or persons who have no religious belief.[157] A further area where specific exemption may be regarded as appropriate is that of adoption and foster care of children. The RRA and FETO both contain exemptions for "anything done by a person as a participant in arrangements under which he (for reward or not) takes into his home, and treats as if they were members of his family, children, elderly persons, or persons requiring a special degree of care and attention". This covers, for example, adoption and foster care.

Q. 22   *Should there be an exemption allowing religious bodies to discriminate on other grounds, such as sex or sexual orientation, where this is necessary and appropriate to comply with the doctrines of the religion or to avoid offending the religious susceptibilities of a significant number of its followers?*

Q.23   *Are there any grounds on which such bodies should not be allowed to discriminate irrespective of the doctrines of their religion, such as race?*

8.16   The discussion above has focused on exemptions from discrimination on the grounds of religion. How far should religious belief provide a justification for discrimination on other grounds, such as sex or sexual orientation? Should a business which claims to have a "Christian ethos" be able to refuse employment to anyone whom it believes violates that ethos for example because of their homosexuality? The issue can be framed in terms of a conflict of rights, between the right to freedom of religion and the right to be free from discrimination on other grounds. This was an issue that was

154 Anti-Discrimination Act 1991 (Qld), s.48.
155 Op. Cit. s. 80.
156 Op. Cit. s. 90.
157 ESA, s. 9(1)(a).

raised during the passage through Parliament of the Human Rights Bill. As a consequence of this concern, the HRA 1998 requires courts to have particular regard to the right to freedom of thought, conscience and religion in the determination of any question arising under the Act that might affect the exercise by a religious organisation of that convention right.[158] As noted above (para 8.9) article 4(2) of the employment directive allows a state to provide an exemption for a difference of treatment based on religion or belief for an organisation the ethos of which is based on religion or belief. But the subsection also provides that it 'should not justify discrimination on another ground'. It is not clear whether the use of the term 'should not' rather than 'shall not' is of any significance.

8.17   Any legislation needs to define carefully to whom such a right to discriminate would belong. In Australia the Victorian *Equal Opportunities Act 1995* does not apply "to discrimination by a person against another person if the discrimination is necessary for the first person to comply with the person's genuine religious beliefs or principles".[159] This approach gives maximum effect to a person's freedom of religion but may undermine the broader principle of equality.

8.18   In 1998 the Australian Human Rights and Equal Opportunity Commission published a detailed report on freedom of religion that weighed up the arguments for and against a general right to discriminate on the basis of conscience and religious belief. The report made a distinction between private and public spheres of activity. It argued that while, as a general rule, in their private lives people should be able to shape their actions on the basis of their religious and other beliefs, this was not appropriate in public life "where the state has a much clearer role in ensuring that people do not exercise their rights in a manner that infringes, unduly upon the rights and freedoms of others and that all people have basic guarantees of physical integrity, equality of opportunity and freedom from discrimination and injustice."[160] Employment, it concluded, clearly fell within the ambit of public life, thus justifying legislative guarantees by the state. It recommended a limited exemption for religious organisations:

It should apply only to employment of people by religious institutions and should be limited to discrimination that is required by the tenets and doctrines of the religion, is not arbitrary and is consistently applied.[161]

---

158 HRA 1998, s. 13.
159 s. 77.
160 *Article 18 – Freedom of Religion and Belief,* (Human Rights and Equal Opportunity Commission, 1998), p. 108.
161 Ibid. at p. 111.

Clearly, some forms of discrimination, such as racial discrimination, by a religious body would be unacceptable. But the SDA contains an exemption for religious bodies allowing them to "discriminate in relation to sex where employment is limited to one sex so as to comply with doctrines of the religion or avoid offending the religious susceptibilities of a significant number of its followers".[162]

8.19   One particularly difficult issue is the extent to which religious organisations can discriminate on the grounds of sexual orientation. Providing an exemption that allows religious organisations to discriminate on the grounds of sexual orientation may be regarded as an endorsement of those beliefs. Alternatively, it may be regarded not as endorsement, but as an accommodation of those beliefs. Dr. Robert Wintemute suggests that there should be a specific exemption for sexual orientation discrimination by religious institutions similar to that for sex found in the SDA and that it should not be extended to cover all employees of religious institutions (other than ministers of religion), such as teachers, secretaries, caretakers, doctors and nurses in schools run by religious institutions.[163]

8.20   Particular issues arise in relation to exemptions from the legislation for religious schools. The approach in Northern Ireland, reflecting the particular sectarian issues in that jurisdiction, is to exclude schools entirely from the FETO, so they are free to discriminate in respect of teachers from the Protestant and Roman Catholic communities.[164] Article 15(2) of the employment directive has expressly preserved this exemption. In Scotland the management of denominational schools is regulated by the *Education (Scotland) Act 1980*.[165] Section 21 of the Act provides that 'a teacher appointed to any post on the staff of any such school by the education authority...shall be required to be approved as regards his religious belief and character by representatives of the church or denominational body in whose interest the school has been conducted'. Employment in religious schools in England and Wales in regulated by the *School Standards Framework Act 1998*. Section 59 of the Act provides firstly that, in community, secular foundation or voluntary or special schools, no one can be disqualified from employment by reasons of his religious opinions, or of attending or omitting to attend religious worship.[166] But s.60 provides that foundation or voluntary schools that have a "religious character" can give preference in employment, remuneration and

162 SDA, s. 19.
163 R. Wintemute, Inclusion of Sexual Orientation Discrimination in UK Anti-Discrimination Legislation, (Working Paper No. 7) (Cambridge, Centre for Public Law, 1999).
164 FETO, art. 71.
165 As amended by the Self-Governing Schools (Scotland) Act 1989 (c39).
166 School Standards and Framework Act 1998, s. 59.

promotion to teachers "whose religious beliefs are in accordance with the tenets" of that religion.[167] Furthermore, "regard may be had, in connection with the termination of the employment of any teacher at that school, to any conduct on his part which is incompatible with the precepts, or with the upholding of the tenets, of the religion or religious denomination so specified".[168] The provisions do not extend to cover employment beyond teaching.[169] The House of Lords Committee indicated that these provisions go beyond those permitted by a "genuine occupational qualification" found in the Article 13 draft employment directive.[170] Responding to these concerns the Government said that they were negotiating to "ensure that the employment directive would permit s.60 of the *Schools Standards and Framework Act 1998* to be maintained".[171] The final text of the employment directive was amended to ensure that the directive did not prejudice the rights of religious schools (above, 8.9, 8.12). The directive as amended "allows Member States considerable latitude in implementing its provisions in relation to staff policies of religious organisations. In particular the agreed text allows the UK to protect the right of church schools to give preference to teachers of their faith in line with the provisions of the *Schools Standards and Framework Act 1998.*"[172]

---

167 Ibid. s. 60(5).
168 Ibid. s. 60(6).
169 Ibid. s. 60(7).
170 House of Lords, *supra* n. 49, at para 188.
171 HL Deb, 30 June 2000, c. 1239.
172 HC 6 November 2000, WA 38

9.   Reasonable accommodation

9.1   This section examines in more detail the concept of reasonable accommodation of religious practice (see para. 6.8 to 6.10 above). Rules, requirements, and practices of employers and providers of goods and services may conflict with a person's religious practice or requirements. Accommodating religious belief is closely connected with the right to manifest religion or belief, as it is usually the manifestation or practice of a religion or belief that needs to be accommodated. The case law of the ECHR on Article 9 (see para 1.12) and of the US Supreme Court under the first amendment to the US constitution provides an indication of some of the issues that may arise in relation to the manifestation of religious belief that are also relevant to reasonable accommodation in the sphere of employment and the provision of goods and services.

9.2   Firstly, what approach should be taken to determining whether a practice is a religious practice? Secondly, what factors should be taken into account in determining whether the employer has met the duty? Thirdly, what are the key areas in which the duty to accommodate religious practice will arise? Fourthly, what are the possible options in such situations? Finally, on whom should the duty fall?

Q. 24   *What approach should be taken in deciding:*
- *If an employee's practice is a manifestation of a religion or belief*
- *If an employer's practice or policy conflicts with the employee's religious practice?*

9.3   A duty on employers, public authorities or schools to accommodate religious practices requires some method of determining whether an act constitutes a religious practice. Should the test be purely subjective, that is a declaration by the person concerned that the conduct in question is a religious practice, a manifestation of his or her belief? The European Commission for Human Rights prefers to take an objective approach, determining for itself whether an act is a manifestation of a person's belief rather than accepting a declaration by the person concerned that their conduct is a manifestation of their belief. In the *Arrowsmith*[173] case the applicant argued that under Article 9 she had a right to hand out leaflets to soldiers advocating that they should not serve in Northern

---

173   *Arrowsmith* v UK (1978) 19 DR 5; (1978) 3 EHRR 110.

Ireland because this was a manifestation of her pacifist beliefs. The Commission held that "when actions of individuals do not actually express the belief concerned they cannot be considered to be as such protected by Article 9(1), even when they are motivated by it". The Commission has also rejected attempts by conscientious objectors to prevent payment of taxes that may be used on military expenditure. It held that only acts "which are aspects of the practice of a religion or belief in a generally recognised form are protected by Article 9"[174] Van Dijk and van Hoof argue that an objective approach to this question is inevitable even if problematic:

[A] restrictive interpretation may in general be unavoidable. A legal system consisting of general binding rules cannot afford to leave to (the subjective convictions of) [a] person the answer to the question whether a person manifests his religion or belief and can rely on Article 9. It should answer the question itself on the basis of objective criteria, primarily related to the outward appearance of the expression.

However, for less known minorities who are not linked up with one of the world religions or ideologies this entails the danger that a behaviour will only be considered the expression of a belief, in case a sufficient resemblance can be found with the known patterns of familiar spiritual movements.[175]

9.4   The European Court of Human Rights took a similar approach when deciding if a rule conflicted with a person's beliefs or religious practice. In the cases of *Valsamis v. Greece*[176] and *Efstratiou v. Greece*[177] the applicants, who were Jehovah's Witnesses, complained that a rule allowing schools to require pupils, under threat of a disciplinary penalty, to take part in the National Day Parade, was in violation of their freedom to manifest their pacifist beliefs. The Court and Commission rejected their applications. The Court held that it could "discern nothing, either in the purpose of the parade or in the arrangements for it, which could offend the applicants' pacifist conviction". Other commentators have argued that there are many dangers in attempting to substitute a court's own interpretation of a particular set of beliefs to that of their holder.[178]

---

174 Appl. 10358/83, *C. v. the United Kingdom*, D&R 37 (1984), p. 142.
175 P. van Dijk and G.J.H. van Hoof, *Theory and Practice of the European Convention on Human Rights*, (The Hague, Kluwer Law International, 3rd ed. 1998), at p. 550.
176 Judgement of 18 December 1996; Comm report, 6.7.95.
177 Judgement of 18 December 1996; Comm report, 11.4.96.
178 S. Stavros, *Freedom of religion and claims for exemption from generally applicable, neutral laws: Lessons from across the Pond?* (Council of Europe, 1998), at p. 7.

9.5   By contrast to the ECHR, the US Supreme Court has held that it is not within the power of the judiciary to question a litigants' interpretation of their religious claim except where the claim "is so bizarre, so clearly non-religious in motivation, as not to be entitled to protection under the Free Exercise Clause".[179] Thus the Supreme Court does not normally question the litigant's claim that engaging in a particular activity would be contrary to his or her religious belief. Under the Ontario Human Rights Commission's policy on creed, personal religious beliefs, practices or observances are protected, even if they are not essential elements of the creed, provided they are sincerely held.

9.6   Will legislation that covers atheism and agnosticism give rise to calls for reasonable accommodation in the same way as religion? Greenwalt argues that "upon closer examination of reasons for action that do not derive from ordinary religious beliefs, we discover that comparatively few claims to perform acts actually derive from atheism and agnosticism".[180] A central part of Greenwalt's argument is that all non-religious reasons for actions by an atheist are not automatically "atheist" reasons. Claims for exemptions from ordinary laws that are based closely on atheism and agnosticism might be so rare as not to require a specific duty of reasonable accommodation

Q. 25   *What factors should be taken into account in determining if the duty has been complied with?*

9.7   The DDA introduced the concept of reasonable adjustment in UK discrimination law (para.6.8 above). In relation to employment it places a duty on employers to take such steps, as it is reasonable, in all the circumstances of the case, to prevent a disabled person from being at a substantial disadvantage compared to a person who is not disabled.[181] The Act gives examples of steps that an employer may have to take to comply with the duty and sets out the factors that need to be taken into account in deciding whether it is reasonable for an employer to have to take a particular step. These include the extent to which taking the step would prevent the effect; the extent to which it is practicable for the employer to take the step; the financial and other costs involved in taking the step and the extent to which it would disrupt any activities; the extent of the employer's financial and other resources; and the availability to the employer of financial and other assistance with respect to taking the step.[182] This is amplified by codes of practice.

---

179   *Thomas v. Review Board of the Indiana Employment Security Decision*, 67 L Ed 2d 624, 632, cited in S. Stavros, *supra* n.1/8, at p. 7.

180   Greenwalt, *supra* n. 80, at p. 1464.

181   DDA, s. 6(1).

182   DDA, s. 6(4).

9.8   There may be factors which should not be taken into account in determining if a duty to accommodate has been complied with. In the USA, the EEOC guidelines note that the assumption that many more people, with the same religious practice of the person being accommodated, may also need accommodation is not evidence of undue hardship. The Ontario Human Rights Commission guideline on their code provides that in no circumstances should discriminatory customer preferences or those of co-workers be considered valid factors when evaluating whether or not an accommodation measure will create undue hardship. However undue hardship would be shown where a variance from a bona fide seniority system is necessary in order to accommodate an employee's religious practices when doing so would deny another employee his or her job or shift preference guaranteed by that system.[183]

Q. 26   *On whom should the duty to accommodate fall?*

9.9   Accommodation may require changes to employment practice that have been agreed in the terms of a collective bargaining agreement. To ensure that accommodation is possible in this situation the duty may need to apply not only to the employer but to unions. In *Central Okanagan School District No. 23 v. Renaud*[184] the Supreme Court of Canada noted that although the principle of equal liability applies, the employer has charge of the workplace and will be in a better position to formulate measures of accommodation. The employer, therefore, can be expected to initiate the process of taking measures to accommodate an employee. Nevertheless, the Court held that this does not absolve a union of its duty to put forward alternative measures that are available. In short, when a union is a co-discriminator with an employer it shares the obligation to remove or alleviate the source of the discriminatory effect. Unions may be liable in two situations:

           ...first, [the union] may cause or contribute to the discrimination by participating in the formulation of the work rule that has a discriminatory effect on the complainant. This will generally be the case if the rule is a provision in the collective agreement; second, a union may be liable if it impedes the reasonable efforts of an employer to accommodate.[185]

183   US Code of Federal Regulation, Title 29, Guidelines on Discrimination because of Religion, s.1605.
184   *Central Okanagan School District No. 23 v. Renaud* (1992), 16 CHRR D/425, Supreme Court of Canada. The British Columbia *Human Rights Act* which was in force at the time did not mention the duty to accommodate explicitly. The principle reached by the Supreme Court of Canada in *Renaud*, namely, that the union as well as the employer has a duty to accommodate short of undue hardship, applies *a fortiori* to the Ontario *Human Rights Code* which explicitly imposes a duty to accommodate, short of undue hardship.
185   *Supra*, n.184, at D/436 - D/437.

9.10   In *Gohm v. Domtar*[186] the employer agreed to accommodate Mrs. Gohm by rescheduling her to work Sunday instead of Saturday, provided she agreed not to receive premium pay for Sunday work as required by the collective agreement. The union blocked the employer's attempt. In finding that the union had discriminated against the complainant, the Ontario Divisional Court set out the concept of "equal partnership":

Discrimination in the workplace is everybody's business. There can be no hierarchy of responsibility...companies, unions and persons are all in a primary and equal position in a single line of defence against all types of discrimination. To conclude otherwise would fail to afford to the Human Rights Code the broad purposive intent that is mandated.[187]

Q. 27   How should employers accommodate religious observance?

9.11   Among the tools available to employers to facilitate requests for accommodation are: rules for granting annual leave, time off in lieu and unpaid leave. In the USA, the EEOC highlight some of the ways in which religious practices can be accommodated:[188]

(i) Voluntary Substitutes and "Swaps"

Reasonable accommodation without undue hardship is generally possible where a voluntary substitute with substantially similar qualifications is available. One means of substitution is the voluntary swap. The securing of a substitute can be left entirely up to the individual seeking the accommodation. [However], the obligation to accommodate may require that employers and labour organisations facilitate the securing of a voluntary substitute with substantially similar qualifications. Some means of doing this which employers and labour organisations could consider are: to publicise policies regarding accommodation and voluntary substitution; to promote an atmosphere in which such substitutions are favourably regarded; to provide a central file, bulletin board or other means for matching voluntary substitutes with positions for which substitutes are needed.

---

186 (1982), 89 DLR (4th) 305 (Ont. Div. Ct.).
187 *Ibid.* at 312.
188 Code of Federal Regulation, Title 29 vol. 4 part 1605 – Guidelines on Discrimination because of Religion.

(ii) Flexible Scheduling

One means of providing reasonable accommodation for the religious practices of employees or prospective employees which employers and labour organisations should consider is the creation of a flexible work schedule for individuals requesting accommodation. The following list is an example of areas in which flexibility might be introduced: flexible arrival and departure times; floating or optional holidays; flexible work breaks; use of lunch time in exchange for early departure; staggered work hours; and permitting an employee to make up time lost due to the observance of religious practices.

(iii) Lateral Transfer and Change of Job Assignments

When an employee cannot be accommodated either as to his or her entire job or an assignment within the job, employers and labour organisations should consider whether or not it is possible to change the job assignment or give the employee a lateral transfer.

Q. 28   *In relation to which religious practices or observances are questions of reasonable accommodation likely to arise? How should such practices and observances be accommodated?*

9.12   The most common areas in which employers may be required to accommodate religious observance and practice that can be identified are: dress codes, break polices, recruitment and job applications; flexible scheduling, rescheduling and religious leave. It may be useful here to consider the options for accommodation in relation to some of these issues.

(i) Dress Codes

9.13   The HREOC guidelines suggest allowing employees to wear head coverings required by religious practice such as yarmulkes, turbans and hijabs as well as allowing Christian employees to wear a cross around their neck or pinned on their clothes.[189] Religious dress may conflict with health and safety requirements.[190] Health and safety considerations may be one of the factors in determining whether accommodation is reasonable. The employers may be required to see whether health and safety gear can be modified to permit the person to wear the religious dress safely.

---

189   Human Rights and Equal Opportunities Commission, *supra* n. 150, p. 9.
190   *Panesar v. Nestle-Co* [1980] IRLR 64, CA.

(ii) Break policies and observance of prayer times

9.14   The Association of Muslim Lawyers argues that reasonable accommodation should include the right to an extended lunch break on Fridays so as to enable employees to attend the collective *Jumu'a* prayers, provided that the extra time spent in such a prayer break is made up during the course of the week.[191] Similarly, employees should be able to pray in their workplace provided that the time spent on such prayers is made up either at the beginning or at the end of the workday.[192] Where possible this may require the provision of space for prayers. There should be flexibility in relation to commencement and finishing times as well as the opportunity to work reduced lunch hours where an employee is observing a fast. Any arrangements of this kind would have to be compatible with the requirements of the Working Time Regulations 1998, S.I. 1998/1833 in respect of the maximum length of the working day and week, and for rest breaks and holidays.

(iii) Recruitment and job applications

9.15   The HREOC guidelines suggest that job application forms and interviews should not contain questions about availability for work that are asked in a manner that reveals the applicant's creed. Nor should questions be designed to reveal that religious requirements might conflict with the prospective employer's work schedule or workplace routine. There should not be inquiries as to religious affiliation, places of worship or customs observed.[193]

(iv) Religious leave

9.16   Bradford City Council has produced a *Code of Practice for Managers on Religious and Cultural Needs*. In relation to religious holidays it recommends that managers should as a matter of practice speak to staff at the commencement of the leave year, or when an individual joins a department to ascertain their religious leave requests, if any, for the coming year. Staff may sometimes wish to work over other public holidays in place of their own religious festivals. In considering such requests the Code of Practice suggests the following be taken into consideration:
- The availability and access of the work location
- The safety and security of the workplace
- The ability to verify that work has been completed
- The financial viability.

191   Association of Muslim Lawyers, *supra* n. 146, at p. 5.
192   Ibid.
193   Human Rights and Equal Opportunity Commission (2000), *supra* n. 150, at p. 9.

(v) Planning policies

9.17   Some local authorities have adopted changes in planning policy to recognise that mosques, gudwaras and temples do not function like traditional churches. The Association of Muslim Lawyers has also argued for a relaxation of parking restrictions around Mosques during Id and Friday prayer times. Such restrictions, they note, are given around churches on Sundays and at Christmas and Easter.[194]

---

194   Association of Muslim Lawyers, *supra* n. 146, at p. 5.

10.   A duty to promote religious equality?

Q. 29   *Should there be a duty on public authorities to promote religious equality?*

10.1   The *Race Relations (Amendment) Act 2000* places a duty on public authorities in respect of racial equality. Section 2 of the Act replaces section 71 of the RRA with a new provision which provides that specified public authorities "shall, in carrying out its functions, have due regard to the need (a) to eliminate unlawful racial discrimination and (b) to promote equality of opportunity and good relations between persons of different racial groups". The CRE may issue codes of practice and has the power to issue and enforce compliance notices where a public authority has failed to comply with this duty. The Government has given a commitment to extend a positive duty on public authorities to cover sex and disability discrimination.[195] If legislation is introduced, should a similar duty apply in respect of religious equality? Such a duty now exists under the *Northern Ireland Act 1998*, s.75, which lays down that "a public authority shall in carrying out its functions relating to Northern Ireland have due regard to the need to promote equality of opportunity between persons of different religious belief". Mainstreaming religious equality policies through a public duty would prevent the issue being marginalized. Under the HRA public authorities are already under a duty not to discriminate on grounds of religion in relation to convention rights. A positive duty would require public authorities to consider the impact of their policies on religious communities as well as having regard to the need to set goals and targets and to review and implement their actions. It may also encourage greater participation by communities that feel they face religious discrimination in the decision-making process.

10.2   Placing such a duty on public authorities raises the further issues of which public bodies would be covered? The Race Relations (Amendment) Act and the NIA have opted for having defined lists of public authorities in contrast to the HRA s.6(3) which does not define a public authority except to include a court or tribunal and also "any persons certain of whose functions are functions of a public nature." The *advantage* of a defined list is that it removes the need for litigation to decide whether an authority is subject to the duty, and creates greater certainty. Public bodies that are not specified are still subject to the duty not to discriminate on grounds of religion or belief under the Article 13 employment directive.

---

195   Cabinet Office, Equality Statement, 30 November 1999.

Q.30   *Should there be a duty on private sector employers to promote religious equality?*

10.3   The FETO imposes positive duties on employers with more than 10 employees to monitor their workforces, and permits affirmative action in order to secure fair participation in employment by members of the Protestant and Roman Catholic communities in Northern Ireland (see paras.1-5 and 1.6 above). The Independent Review of the Enforcement of UK Anti-Discrimination Legislation has proposed that every employer in the UK with more than 10 employees should be required to conduct a periodical review (once every three years) of its employment practices for the purpose of determining whether members of ethnic minorities, women and disabled persons are enjoying, or are likely to continue to enjoy fair participation in employment in the undertaking.[196] However, this proposal does not extend to religious groups.

Q.31   *Should the legislation allow positive action to ensure equal treatment for religious groups?*

10.4   The Article 13 employment directive provides in Article 7 that:

With a view to ensuring full equality in practice, the principle of equal treatment shall not prevent any Member State from maintaining or adopting specific measures to prevent or compensate for disadvantages linked to any of the grounds referred to in Article 1.

The SDA and RRA do not permit "reverse discrimination" in favour of women or ethnic minorities. However, as an exception to the general non-discrimination principle they permit certain positive measures to encourage workers and potential workers and to provide training for workers from under-represented groups. Case studies for the Independent Review revealed that these provisions are little used and are out of date.[197] The Review proposed in their place a general exception for positive action in the case of ethnic groups, women and disabled persons along the lines now envisaged in the Article 13 employment directive. The proposal did not extend to religious groups, and it may be thought that a duty to make reasonable adjustments would be the most effective way of preventing or compensating for disadvantages linked to religious discrimination (see section 9, above).

---

196   Hepple, Coussey and Choudhury, *supra* n. 1, paras.3.37 to 3.39 and Recommendation 28.
197   Op. Cit., paras 2.48 and 2.49.

11.   Enforcement of religious discrimination legislation

Q.32   *Should there be an organisation with responsibility for enforcement of religious discrimination legislation, and if so who should have this responsibility*
- *The Commission for Racial Equality*
- *A new Commission for Religious Relations*
- *A single Equality Commission dealing with all grounds of discrimination*
- *A Human Rights Commission?*

11.1   The existing anti-discrimination legislation in the UK provides for commissions whose role it is to undertake strategic enforcement of the legislation, support and assistance to those experiencing discrimination as well a wider educational and promotional role. Although the Article 13 employment directive does not specifically require a body to be designated for this purpose, consideration should to be given as to which, if any body should be responsible for enforcement and promotional roles. Four options will be considered here. **Firstly**, the role could be given to one of the existing commissions, the most likely candidate being the CRE. **Secondly**, a separate commission could be set up. **Thirdly**, there could be a new single Equality Commission covering all grounds of unlawful discrimination. **Fourthly**, there could be a Human Rights Commission either on its own or working with the appropriate equality commission.

11.2   Attaching the duty of enforcing religious discrimination legislation to the CRE would be a logical extension of its present activities, particularly because of the growth of "cultural" racism, and the blurred lines between race and religion. As noted earlier, the RRA has been used for protection against discrimination by some religious communities that are able to bring themselves within the definition of ethnic group and as a form of indirect racial discrimination. The relationship between racial and religious discrimination is complex and overlapping. Placing responsibility for religious discrimination with the CRE would avoid the need to go to two bodies in cases where it is unclear whether the discrimination is on the grounds of race or religion. On the other hand, there is a danger that claims of religious discrimination would be marginalized within an organisation with an established tradition and experience in tackling racial discrimination. This may be particularly important in cases where there is no element of racial discrimination.

11.3   The second option is to have a new Commission dealing only with religious equality. Such a commission may provide symbolic value in the recognition of the importance of religious discrimination. It would be able to focus its energies and resources to tackling religious discrimination. The main *disadvantage* is that this would be yet another commission operating in the area of discrimination. Given the complex relationship between racial and religious discrimination much of its work would overlap with that of the CRE. Setting up a new separate Commission would take time and also require considerable extra resources

11.4   The Independent Review of Enforcement of UK Anti-Discrimination Legislation[198] has proposed that there should be a single Equality Commission covering all grounds of unlawful discrimination, including religion. This would follow the precedent in Northern Ireland where the enforcement of the religious discrimination legislation and the new duty on public authorities to promote equality of opportunity has been transferred to the single Equality Commission which also deals with discrimination on grounds of race, sex and disability. The main *advantages* would be to give the principle of equality a higher status, the commission would speak with a single, strong voice on all equality issues and could give consistent advice, would be able to deal more effectively with multiple discrimination cases and avoid duplication of resources. Case studies conducted for the Independent Review indicated strong employer support for a single agency. The main *disadvantage* is seen by some as the possible swamping of religious issues by other interest groups. This argument assumes that the function of a commission is to operate as a pressure group for particular interests. An alternative view is that this is the function of non-governmental organisations, and that a commission is a governmental body concerned with enforcement and general promotion.

11.5   The Institute of Public Policy Research[199] has set out the case for a Human Rights Commission in Great Britain. The functions of such a commission would include the review of legislation, scrutiny of draft legislation, giving advice and assistance to individuals and guidance to organisations, conducting inquiries and investigations and generally promoting all human rights. Such a commission could exist alongside an equality commission or commissions, as in Northern Ireland.

198   Hepple, Coussey and Choudhury (2000), supra n. 1, paras. 2.88-2.91.
199   S. Spencer and I. Bynoe, *A Human Rights Commission: The Options for Great Britain and Northern Ireland*, (London, IPPR, 1998).

Q.32   What other enforcement measures are required?

11.6   Whichever of these options, if any, is chosen consideration may also need to be given to administrative measures that may be adopted to support the enforcement of legislation tackling religious discrimination. These might include the issuing of a code of best practice for employers and providers of goods, services and facilities in relation to the accommodation of religious practice. The Better Regulation Task Force has urged the Government to promote equality practices among contractors and suppliers to the public sector.[200] The Independent Review of UK Anti-Discrimination Law recommends that equality standards be included among the core performance indicators for the purposes of compliance with the duty to secure best value.[201]

11.7   The Article 13 employment directive requires Member States to promote dialogue between the social partners with a view to fostering equal treatment, including through the monitoring of workplace practices, collective agreements, codes of conduct and through research or exchange of experiences and good practices. A Code of Practice on Religious Equality could give guidance on all these matters. Employers' organisations and trade unions could themselves initiate dialogue and action on these matters between themselves and also with other non-governmental organisations.

11.8   The enforcement of individual claims of religious discrimination would no doubt follow the same lines as enforcement of other anti-discrimination legislation, in particular through the employment tribunals in employment cases. Here attention may be drawn to Article 10 of the employment directive on the burden of proof and, more generally, to the recommendations of the Independent Review on measures to make procedures and remedies more effective.[202]

200   The Better Regulations Task Force, *Review of Anti-Discrimination Legislation* (London, Central Office of Information, 1999), pp. 25-26.
201   Hepple, Coussey, Choudhury (2000), *supra* n. 1, at para 3.75.
202   Op. Cit., chap.4

Appendix 1   Comparative legislation

Australia

Australian Capital Territory – *Discrimination Act 1991*
s.7(1)(h), s.11 (employee's religious practice); s.32 (exemption for religious bodies); s.33 (exemptions for educational institutions conducted for religious purposes); s.44 (exemption for religious workers); s.46 (exemption for religious educational institutions).

Northern Territories of Australia – *Anti-Discrimination Act 1996*
s.19(m) (prohibition of discrimination on the grounds of religious belief or activity); s.24 (failure to accommodate special need); s.43 (exemptions for cultural and religious sites).

Queensland – *Anti-Discrimination Act 1991,*
s.7(1)(h) (prohibits discrimination on the basis of 'religion'); s.29 (exemption for educational or health related institutions with a religious purpose); s.48 (exemption from discrimination in the goods and services for sites of cultural or religious significance); s.80 (exemption from discrimination in disposition of land for sites of cultural and religious significance); s.90 (exemption from discrimination in accommodation for accommodation with religious purposes); s.109 (general exemption regarding religious bodies); s.126 (incitement of racial and religious hatred).

Tasmania – *Anti-Discrimination Act 1998*
s.16(o) and (p) (prohibit discrimination on the grounds of religious belief or affiliation and religious activity); s.19(d) (prohibits incitement of hatred on the grounds of religious belief or affiliation or religious activity); s.51 (exception for employment based on religion); s.52 (exception for participation in religious observance).

Victoria – *Equal Opportunities Act 1995*
s.6 (prohibits discrimination on the grounds of religious belief or activity, this is defined in s.4 as (a) holding or not holding a lawful religious belief or view, (b) engaging in, not engaging in or refusing to engage in a lawful religious activity); s.38 (exceptions from discrimination in education); s.75 exception for religious bodies; s.76 (exception for religious schools); s.77 (exception for religious beliefs and principles).

Western Australia – *Equal Opportunity Act 1984*
Part IV prohibits discrimination on grounds of religious or political conviction.

Canada

Federal Level – *Canadian Human Rights Act, R.S.C. 1985, c.H-6*
s.3(1), prohibits discrimination on the grounds of religion; s.15(1)(a), exemption where discriminatory requirement is a bona-fide occupational requirement; s.15(1)(g), discrimination in access to goods, services, facilities, or accommodation or access thereto or occupancy of any commercial premises or residential accommodation is permitted where there is a bona fide justification for that denial or differentiation; s.15(2), to be a bona fide occupational qualification or a bona fide justification, it must be established that the needs of an individual or a class of individuals affected would impose undue hardship on the person who would have to accommodate those needs, considering health, safety and cost.

Alberta – *Human Rights, Citizenship and Multiculturalism Act, H-11.7*
The Act prohibits discrimination on the grounds of 'religious belief' in relation to: s.3 (goods services and facilities); s.4 (tenancy); s.8 (advertising); s.10 (membership of unions).

British Columbia – *Human Rights Code 1998, c.210*
Prohibits discrimination on the grounds of 'religion' in the following areas: s.7 (publications); s.8 (accommodation services and facilities); s.9 (purchase of properties); s.10 (tenancy and premises); s.11 (employment advertisements); s.13 (employment) and s.14 (unions and associations).

Manitoba – *Human Rights Code, H175*
s.9(2)(d) (prohibits discrimination on the basis of religion or creed, or religious belief, religious association or religious activity); s.9(1)(d) (definition of discrimination includes failure to make reasonable accommodation); s.14(11) (exception for the lawful and reasonable disciplining of an employee who improperly uses the employment or occupation as a forum for promoting beliefs or values). The code generally allows discrimination if a 'bona fide and reasonable justification exists for the discrimination'.

New Brunswick – *Human Rights Act 1985, c.30*
Prohibits discrimination on the basis of religion.

Nova Scotia – *Human Rights Act 1989, c.214*
 s.5(1) (prohibits discrimination on the grounds of religion); s.6(1)(c)(ii) (exception for employment by non-profit making religious organisations); s.6(1)(c)(iii) (exception for employees engaged by exclusively religious organisations to perform religious duties); s.6(1)(d) (exception for services provided by non-profit religious organisations); s.6(1)(f)

(provides general exception allowing discrimination where it is (i) based on a bona fide qualification, or (ii) a reasonable limit prescribed by law as can be demonstrably justified in a free and democratic society.

Ontario – *Human Rights Code 1990*
Creates a right to equal treatment without discrimination on the grounds of 'creed' in the areas of: s.1 (services, goods and facilities); s.2 (accommodation); s.3 (Contracts); s.5 (Employment); s.11 (constructive discrimination); s.18 (exemption for religious organisations in provision of goods and services); s.24 (exemption for religious organisations in employment).

Prince Edward Island – *Human Rights Act, 1988, H.12*
s(1)(1)(d) and s.13 covers 'religion and creed'; s.6(4)(c) (exception for employment by religious organisations); s.10(2) (exception from discrimination in provision of services by a non-profit making religious organisation 'operated primarily to foster the welfare of the religious group').

Quebec – *Charter of Rights and Freedoms, c. C-12*
s.10 (prohibition of discrimination on the grounds of 'religion'); s.20 (general exemption for religious organisations holds that 'a distinction, exclusion or preference based on the aptitudes or qualifications required for an employment or justified by the...religious...nature of a non-profit institution...is deemed to be non-discriminatory').

European Union

Austria – Article 7.1 of the constitution

Belgium – Article 10, 11, and 191 of the Constitution contains a general principle of equality.

Denmark – Article 70 of the constitution

Finland – Section 5 of the constitution

France – Article 2 of the constitution

Germany – Article 3 of the constitution

Greece – Article 4.1, 5.1 and 5.3 of the constitution

Ireland – Article 40 of the constitution contains a general principle of equality. *Employment Equality Act 1998* prohibits discrimination in employment; *Equal Status Act 2000* prohibits discrimination in the provision of goods, services and facilities

Italy – Article 3 of the constitution

Luxembourg – Article 11 of the constitution

The Netherlands – Article 1 of the constitution; The *Equal Treatment Act 1984* prohibits discrimination in employment and the provision of goods, services and facilities.

Portugal – Article 13 of the constitution

Spain – Article 14 of the constitution

Sweden – Chapter 2 Article 1.6, 15 and 20.6 of the constitution

New Zealand

Bill of Rights Act 1990,
s. 13 (freedom of thought, conscience and religion); s. 15 (right to manifestation of religion and belief); s.19 (freedom from discrimination); s. 20 (rights of minorities).

Human Rights Act 1993
s.21(1) prohibits discrimination on the grounds of religion or ethical belief in the areas of employment, accommodation, education and goods and services. Section 28 exceptions for the purposes of religion.

United States of America

The First Amendment of the US Constitution provides that Congress may neither establish a religion nor prohibit its free exercise. The US Supreme Court has held that, under the establishment clause, federal, state and local government may not, directly or indirectly demonstrate any preference for any church or any religious belief. Article VI of the US Constitution prohibits any requirement for an office holder to belong to or adhere to any particular religious faith. *Civil Rights Act 1964* prohibits religious discrimination in employment, education and accommodation.

International

African Charter on Human and People's Rights 1981
Article 2 prohibits discrimination on the basis of religion in relation to the Charter rights and freedoms. Article 8 provides that 'freedom of conscience, the profession and free practice of religion shall be guaranteed'.

American Convention on Human Rights (1969)
Article 12 (right to freedom of conscience and religion).

European Convention on Human Rights and Fundamental Freedoms (1950)
Article 9 (the rights to freedom of thought, conscience and religion); article 14 (prohibits discrimination on the basis of religion in relation to Convention rights).

The European Social Charter
The European Social Charter is the counter part to the European Convention on Human Rights. While the ECHR covers civil and political rights the ESC 1961 is a binding instrument covering economic and social rights. The UK signed the Charter in 1961 and ratified it the following year. The preamble to the Charter requires the enjoyment of social rights to be enjoyed without distinction on grounds of religion.

The International Covenant on Civil and Political Rights (1966)
Article 2(1) prohibits discrimination in relation to convention rights on the basis of religion. Article 26 provides that the law shall 'prohibit any discrimination and guarantee to all persons equal and effective protection against discrimination on any ground such as…religion'.

The International Covenant on Economic, Social and Cultural Rights
Article 2(2) requires State Parties to guarantee the Covenant rights without discrimination as to religion.

Convention on the Rights of the Child 1989
Article 2 requires State Parties to ensure that the rights set forth in the Convention are extended to all children within their jurisdiction 'without discrimination of any kind irrespective of the child's or his or her parent's or legal guardian's religion'. State Parties are under a duty to 'take all appropriate measures to ensure that the child is protected against all forms of discrimination or punishment on the basis of the…beliefs of the child's parents, legal guardians, or family members.

ILO Convention 111 Concerning Discrimination in Respect of Employment and Occupation 1958
Article 1(b) prohibits discrimination on the grounds of religion.

Appendix 2

List of religions

The following categories of religion are listed in the Home Office Prisons Statistics. This provides an indication of the religions that might be included in a list of religions.

Anglican
    Anglican
    Church of Wales
    Church of England
    Church of Ireland
    Episcopalian

Roman Catholic

Free Church
    Baptist
    Celestial Church of God
    Church of Scotland
    Congregational
    Methodist
    Non-Conformist
    Pentecostal
    Presbyterian
    Quaker
    Salvation Army
    United Reformed Church
    Welsh Independent

Buddhist

Hindu

Jewish

Mormon

Muslim

Sikh

Others
    Protestant
    Jehovah's Witnesses
    Greek/Russian Orthodox
    Christian Scientist
    Seven Day Adventist
    Ethiopian Orthodox
    Spiritualist
    Christadelphian
    Other Christian religions
    Other non-Christian religions

RDS Publications

Requests for Publications

Copies of our publications and a list of those currently available may be obtained from:

> Home Office
> Research, Development and Statistics Directorate
> Communications Development Unit
> Room 201, Home Office
> 50 Queen Anne's Gate
> London SW1H 9AT
> Telephone: 020 7273 2084 (answerphone outside of office hours)
> Facsimile: 020 7222 0211
> E-mail: publications.rds@homeoffice.gsi.gov.uk

alternatively

why not visit the RDS website at
>   Internet: http://www.homeoffice.gov.uk/rds/index.html

where many of our publications are available to be read on screen or downloaded for printing.